DARK MOUNTAIN

Issue 10 · Uncivilised Poetics · Autumn 2016

The Dark Mountain Project

Published by the Dark Mountain Project 2016
www.dark-mountain.net

ISBN 978-0-9955402-0-0

Editors
Em Strang
Nick Hunt
Cate Chapman

Art Editor
Charlotte Du Cann

Proofreader
Mark Watson

Editorial Assistant
Ava Osbiston

Assistant Reader
Harriet Pierce

Audio Production
Marmaduke Dando

Founders
Dougald Hine
Paul Kingsnorth

Typesetting
Christian Brett, Bracketpress

Printed and bound by
TJ International Ltd.
Padstow

Cover Art
Uncivilised Poetics by Nick Hayes
Crayon

I was given two poems to work from for this front cover, each telling a story of the importance of poetry in the wake of a devastated environment. I wanted to draw an image of time passing, the sun and the moon, the cold spring and warm autumn colours, and give an idea of nature flourishing through the ruins of civilisation. The image of the two silhouetted characters is meant to suggest the function of storytelling, providing a line of communication through past time. And the severed statue head and the Greek urn were references to Shelley and Keats respectively, and their words on poetics and the fall of civilisations.

Text from 'A Ritual to Read to Each Other' by William Stafford (p. 17).

Contents

Issue 10 · Uncivilised Poetics · Autumn 2016

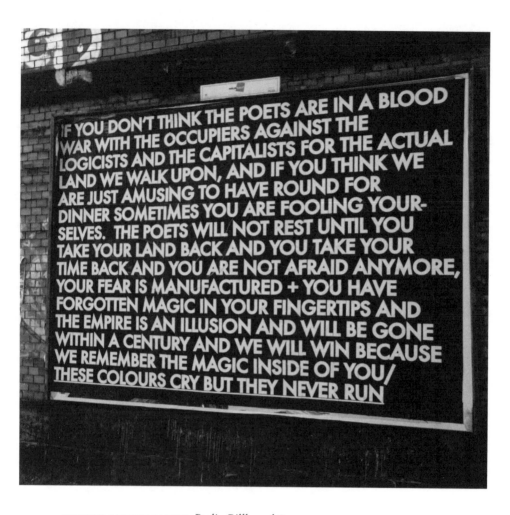

ROBERT MONTGOMERY Berlin Billboard 8

What mad pursuit? What struggle to escape?
– John Keats, 'Ode on a Grecian Urn'

When the forms of an old culture are dying,
the new culture is created by people who
are not afraid to be insecure.
– Rudolf Bahro

There's something dishevelled and unsettling about poetry. In 2016, at a time of escalating global violence and uncertainty, poetry might seem irrelevant. What's the point of poetry when the streets of Syria have been bombed beyond recognition? What's the point of poetry when the permafrost is melting? But poetry matters because it offers an alternative reality – it refuses the logical, reductionist, materialist aspects of industrial culture; aslant, it invites us to feel our way in the dark. And most importantly, it matters because it often fails. Poetry often fails to speak universally, but succeeds in trying over and over again to speak. Poetry is a shabby, uncivilised failure that we badly need in these unravelling times; if for no other reason than as a mirror for our human imperfection.

American poet Adrienne Rich, in her anthology *Arts of the Possible: Essays and Conversations* (2001), asks 'what kind of voice is breaking silence and what kind of silence is being broken?' In this tenth Dark Mountain anthology, our second themed publication, myriad voices continue to break silence on the crumbling narratives of our time: ecological, social and cultural. Many ask what it means to experience a felt sense of the world, when the lives we inhabit are defined by the 'self-congratulatory self-promotion of capitalism', gasping against a backdrop of resource depletion. With our centuries-long reliance on logocentric thinking and being in the world, how do we feel our way to an understanding of what it means to be human today? Poems, resilient and germinal as they are, can forge a path into these questions.

It's true that we don't have to read poems to discover poetry, since it can be found just about anywhere. Poetry isn't necessarily language or the construction of crafted syntax and rhythm. Poetry can be found in the silence, the spontaneous images and realisations that emerge from a creative contemplation of the world: poetry as aware-ness or revelation, from which we gain new insight into ways of seeing and being in the world. But poems are always striving to reveal their poetry and so the more poems we read, the more chance we have of discovering some. It's precisely this chance that *Uncivilised Poetics* is inviting readers to take. This is an anthology of poems, essays, visual art and an audio CD, which urges us, at a time of converging crises, to reimagine ourselves and the world in which we live.

Robert Bringhurst writes about the survival of poetry depending 'to a degree, on the failure of language'; that is, on the failure of language to try to pin down or co-opt poetry. Unlike many things in the 21st century, poetry (as distinct from poems) cannot be bought or sold, locked up or put on display. If there's one thing that remains free of the tentacles of capitalism, free in fact from any system or ideology or marketplace, it's poetry. Not anthologies of poetry – not even this one, uncivilised as it may be – but poetry that equates to an imaginal shift, that moment of awareness or revelation, which Margaret Atwood calls a 'state of free float'.

In 2016, it's true that poems, like most things in our materialist culture, have become business. Not just in the sense that publishers can make money – albeit little – out of successful poets, but in the way in which poets may be tempted to slip more and more towards a kind of formulaic writing; to produce poems which tick all the right boxes in terms of scansion, syntax and poetic strategy. These days there's often praise for the sonnet that doesn't put a single foot wrong, or the esoteric, perhaps hyper-intellectual poem, which only a small coterie can relate to. Not that there's anything wrong with crafting poems – hyper-intellectual or not; the problem is the misperception that the business-like attainment of poetic craft equates to the production of poetry. Federico García Lorca suggested that 'ability is not important, nor technique, nor skill. What matters here is something other.' Technique and skill aside, it's true that without that something other, poems remain at the level of linguistic foreplay, clever *Homo sapiens'* system construction, the bones of something with no wind blowing through it.

Perhaps, in order to participate in poetry, we must open ourselves – writers and readers alike – and realise that poetry is accessible and alive to anyone who waits patiently, listens attentively and responds. Even the simplest poem – such as Najat Abdul Samad's 'If' – can uncover poetry; can, as Lorca suggested, have that 'something other'. Reading and writing poems is a way towards discovering poetry, if we remain open, perhaps even vulnerable, in the face of poetry's power and integrity. It isn't that poets should stop writing poems – on the contrary – but that we come to recognise ourselves as immersive participants, writing with dirt under our fingernails, instead of as 'poets-to-be-watched' in a world that, frankly, has very little to do with poetry at all.

In recognition of the fact that human beings have failed to understand the axiomatic truth that we inhabit this Earth *alongside* other beings, we have chosen to place interrelationship at the heart of this anthology. *Uncivilised Poetics* is woven together to highlight the essential, relational nature of co-existence. Both written and spoken work is gathered to reflect (on) the relationship between species; between genres; between oral and literate, and between *logos* and *mythos*. In a culture which encourages the idea that humans are separate and 'apart from' other beings, and which reinforces an individualistic perception of being, it feels necessary, even urgent, to counter this with the reality of interrelationship. In keeping with this, we've chosen to honour the original languages in which the poems were written: there are inclusions here in Spanish, Japanese, Swedish and Arabic, alongside their translated counterparts.

The *Uncivilised Poetics* CD is the first audio release made to complement a Dark Mountain publication. It includes a mix of well-known poems, accompanied by music and soundings (Robin Robertson; Mairi Campbell reading George Mackay Brown); fiery new poems by Francesca Beard and Mark Rylance; bioacoustics by Bernie Krause, and a sound recording by Peter Cowdrey. The audio component of *Uncivilised Poetics* is intended to celebrate the necessity and potency of oral poetry – not just as a reminder of poetry's origins, but of its performative nature, a form that connects us, amongst other things, to land, myth and dreamtime. Poetry needs to be heard as much as read.

Why 'poetics'? Traditionally, the word refers to the analysis of poetic syntax and form, linguistic techniques. But there's an elasticity in the term that allows it to encompass both poems and poetry, and therefore both poems and other art forms. *Poetics* feels like an exploration rather than a presentation of creative work; there are open-ended questions inherent in its making, rather than a *fait accompli* assertion that here be poetry. *Uncivilised* Poetics because modernity and its colossal ideas are collapsing. The urn has cracked. The work gathered here explores what happens in the gaps, what shape the shards, when the world as we know it fails. A kind of *kintsukuroi* in book/CD form – that careful Japanese art of building a new pot from its broken predecessor; not patching back together, but moving beyond original form to one which embraces flaws, even sees beauty in imperfection.

It's possible to arrange the work in *Uncivilised Poetics* into different categories: ecological poetry; socially-engaged narratives; artistic explorations into the relationship between land and body, human and animal; contemplation of the spiritual and ineffable; ecofeminist calls to act; philosophies of 'the real story' – and none of this would be necessarily incorrect. We could talk about the way in which the contemporary nature poet is turning her attention to an ever more rapidly diminishing natural world in today's technological, consumer capitalist era; or the way in which we have lost touch with the oral poem and its shamanic origins. And we could talk about the radical importance of guerilla poetry in the cities and the mountains. But sometimes such analysis and categorisation seem to lead us away from an appreciation of poetry, no matter what art form it arises in, towards a troublesome pinning down, explaining and controlling – precisely the opposite of what poetry is in the first place. As Bringhurst suggests, it feels like 'one more step in reducing the world to human terms'.

Essentially, *Uncivilised Poetics* is a holding vessel for multiple voices, well-known and new, human and nonhuman, trying at a time of global suffering and loss, to honestly express what is. 'Beauty is truth, truth beauty' but that isn't all we know on Earth and it isn't necessarily all we need to know.

– The Editors,
 August 2016

Dark Mountain would not exist without the support and generosity of its readers. There are many ways to get involved with the project, but the simplest and most direct form of support you can offer is to become a subscriber. For more information, visit: dark-mountain.net/subscribe

The Tree That Became a House

John Haines

They came to live in me
who never lived in the woods before.

They kindled a fire
in my roots and branches,
held out their hands
never cramped by the weight of an axe.

The flames lighted a clearing
in the dark overhead, a sky of wood;
they burned in me a little hollow
like a moon of ash.

I stand here fastened in a living box,
half in my dream life
with finches, wind and fog —

an endless swaying,
divided in the walls that keep them,
in the floors that hold them up,
in the sills they lean upon.

The children look out in wonder
at trees shouldering
black against the starlight;
they speak in whispers,
searching the forest of sleep.

My split heart creaks in the night
around them,
my dead cones drop in silence.

The Persistence of Poetry and
the Destruction of the World Robert Bringhurst

What it pleases us to call the New World is in fact a very old world – just as old, at any rate, as Asia, Europe, and Africa. It is part of the ancient continent of Pangaea, born from the same geological matrix as Europe. Its rivers and forests, and its ecology and geology, were thoroughly developed long before Columbus. And it has been inhabited by thinking, speaking, knowing human beings for several thousand years.

But an inhabited world, with its own philosophical, artistic, scientific and literary traditions, is not what the European conquerors and colonists wanted to find. It is therefore not what they saw. They saw instead an empty world, free and ripe for the taking. They saw a gift of God meant for no-one but themselves.

This deliberate hallucination is still with us, like the star of a Christmas without end.

The European colonists' arrival in the New World marks the escalation of a war that had been fought in Europe and Asia for more than two millennia and continues even now. It is the war between those who think they belong to the world and those who think that the world belongs to them. It is the war between the pagans, who know they are surrounded and outnumbered by the gods, and all the devotees of the number one – one empire, one history, one market, or one God – who nowadays insist on the pre-eminence of everyone for himself: the smallest number one of all.

It is no accident that prophets of monotheism, including Plato and Mohammed, have often banished the poets. These prophets understand that the poet is a pagan and polytheist by nature. In a certain sense, even Dante, Milton, San Juan de la Cruz, Teresa of Ávila,

Gerard Manley Hopkins and T.S. Eliot are pagans. Without admitting it, they seem to understand, like the peoples of the Altiplano of Bolivia and Peru, and like many Native Canadians, that it is best to interpret Christianity as one more form of paganism.

But Mohammed and Plato are poets too in their way, monotheistic and tedious at times, but very much livelier and more pluralistic at others.

The great danger is single-mindedness: reducing things to one perspective, one idea, one overriding rule.

A polytheistic understanding of the world survived in Europe even in the time of the conquistadors, though it was then forced to take a wordless form. Music gave it refuge. It is found in polyphonic music, which is the music of multiple, simultaneous and independent voices. The churches of Europe overflowed with music of this kind in the fifteenth, sixteenth and seventeenth centuries. It did not change the course of history, but it preserved an essential perception of the plurality of being. It preserved the essential, faithful heresy that reality is not of just one mind.

European music of more recent centuries is, for the most part, homophonic. It is the music of one voice that speaks in the names of all and of many voices that answer as one voice.

In the meantime, the conquest continues – in South America, North America, Asia, Australia, and in Europe too. It continues in Bosnia and Herzegovina, where a tradition of oral epic poetry survived from Homer's time until even a few months ago. Now, at this moment, the villages in which those poets lived are rubble and mass graves.

From Alaska to Tierra del Fuego, and from Ireland to Japan, the forests fall and subdivisions replace them. The homes of the gods are supplanted by the houses and garages of human beings. It is hard work, this eviction of the gods and of all the cultures that acknowledge their existence. We keep at it even so.

The Haida poet Skaay refers to human beings as *xhaaydla xitiit ghidaay*: 'plain, ordinary surface birds.' Creatures with more power – killer whales, loons, grebes, sea lions, seals – know how to dive. They pierce the surface, the *xhaaydla* it is called in Haida. If we go with them – if, that is, we are *invited* to go with them – we enter the world of the myths. We come back speaking poetry.

Two thousand kilometres south of the country of the poet Skaay, in the Ruby Mountains, the country of the Paiute, now part of the state of Nevada, there are pines of the species *Pinus aristata*, bristle-cone pines. These trees live longer than any other creatures on the earth. The oldest individuals – not much taller than I am – are 5000 years of age or more. A few years ago, a person who called himself a scientist found in these mountains a pine that might, he thought, be the oldest of all. He cut it down to count its rings. He killed what may indeed have been the oldest living being in the world, to convert it into a statistic. Then he published his report, without the least apology, in a scientific journal.[1]

This is not science. It is one more thoughtless manifestation of the conquest, one more step in reducing the world to human terms.

The American novelist William Faulkner, when he received the Nobel Prize, concluded his address by saying, 'Mankind will not only survive, he will prevail.' I am an admirer of Faulkner, but I think that his prediction is logically impossible. I think that if humanity survives, it can only be because it does *not* prevail, and that if we insist, like Ozymandias, on prevailing, we will surely not survive.

I have been listening to the world for barely half a century. I do not have the wisdom even of a young tree of an ordinary kind. Nevertheless, I have been listening – with eyes, ears, mind, feet, fingertips – and what I hear is poetry.

What does this poetry say? It says that what-is *is*: that the real is real, and that it is alive. It speaks the grammar of being. It sings the polyphonic structure of meaning itself.

In the great ceiling of the Sistine Chapel there are readers rather than writers. The prophets and sibyls scrutinise their folios and scrolls. Nothing is written there that we can read. The great pages in their laps and in their hands reflect what happens as if they were mirrors. In front of these blank mirrors the blind prophets are listening. There is only one writer, Jehoshaphat the scribe, tucked away in the corner with his scrap of paper, listening to those who really listen.

The theme of the ceiling is the poetry of the world, not the glory of the poet.

It is true that the face of Michelangelo is there in the midst of the chapel's big back wall. It is rendered, this self-portrait, as a face still attached to a human hide freshly peeled from someone else's living body. The sculptor is subsumed in his own tale. The listener listens to himself. In the midst of his own vision, the visionary can be seen. But he is peeled. In the midst of that most sculptural of paintings, the image of the sculptor is reduced to two dimensions.

When I was a youngster in school, someone asked me, 'If a tree falls in the forest with no one there to hear it, does it make a sound or not?' The question is demented. If a tree falls in the forest, all the other trees are there to hear it. But if a man cuts down the forest and then cries that he has no food, no firewood, no shade, and that his mind can get no traction, who is going to hear *him*?

Poetry is the language of being: the breath, the voice, the song, the speech of being. It does not need us. We are the ones in need of it. If we haven't learned to hear it, we will also never speak it.

Beings eat one another. This is the fundamental business of the world. It is the whole, not any of its parts, that must prevail, and this whole is always changing. There is no indispensable species, and no indispensable culture. Especially not a culture that dreams of eating without being eaten, and that offers the gods not even the guts or the crumbs.

When he sees his own people destroying the world, what is the poet to say? *Stop*? Or more politely, *Please stop, please*?

All the poets of all times can only say one thing. They can say that what-is is. When he sees his people destroying the world, the poet can say, 'We're destroying the world.' He can say it in narrative or lyric or dramatic or meditative form, tragic or ironic form, short form or long form, in verse or prose. But he cannot lie, as a poet, and offer himself as the saviour. He can believe or not believe that salvation is possible. He can believe in one God or in many gods or in none. He can believe or not believe in belief. But he cannot finally say anything more than the world has told him.

When he sees that, in absolute terms, we human beings are now too numerous – in addition to the fact that we seem too powerful as a species – what is the poet going to do? Pull a trigger? Sing a song of praise to Herod or to Hitler? It is hard to say it to other humans, and humans of course, are loathe to believe it, but this is the fact: human beings have built a world in which humans need to die more and faster than they do. Yet even in this condition, murder is not the answer.

Long ago, in a book of poems protesting the war in Vietnam, I read a simple statement that stays with me. I have not in 30 years been able to find the book again, and I am told that the lines I remember are really quoted from a speech by Martin Luther King. I remember seeing them in a poem, but perhaps the book in which I saw them was published only in my dreams. The lines as I remember them, in any case, are these:

> When one is guided by conscience only,
> there is no other side
> to which one can cross.

There is no other earth to cross to either. There are no new worlds. Paradise will not be our asylum, and our hell will not be anywhere other than here. The world is one, at the same time that it is plural, inherently plural, like the mind. The proof of this plurality is the persistence of poetry in our time. It is extraordinary but true, in the present day, that poetry survives in the voices of humans, just as it does in the voices of all the other species in the world.

Note

1. The first-person account of this event is in Donald R. Currey, 'An Ancient Bristle-cone Pine Stand in Eastern Nevada', *Ecology* 46.4 (Durham, North Carolina, 1965), p. 564–6. Galen Rowell retells the story well in *High and Wild* (San Francisco: Sierra Club, 1979), p. 99–105.

The oak fell without warning
and only you and me
out of all who've ever lived
were there to hear it. The oak fell
with a sound so physical
it flushed out all
those ancestral terrors, those
fluttering undergrowth-dwellers
hidden in the heart.
We rushed outside.
The whole lawn
was a sprawl of branches
reaching out for eighty feet
from the fractured
trunk to the kitchen door.
The torn bark smelled of cumin,
brandy, cloves.

What, years later, I remember,
is the rustling that went on
for half an hour or more:
an ecosystem all astir,

adjusting itself
to a new and terminal axis;
a point in history
held, suspended,
as we clambered among fallen boughs.

I kept asking if you thought
there was a pivot
when its skyward reach
first tipped headlong,
when the hung parliament of cells
at last gained a majority of death.
But life's hidden workings fall
upon us suddenly, or else
the scale of time and place
we live by is a pinpoint
in the surface of the truth.
Like an actor coming into view
from behind the camera,
the world made its entrance
into our lives; like a larva,
hatching and feeding in a pool for months
until, when it breaks the water's
gloss and first unfolds
the rods and banners of its wings,
there's a blur, a flash, and a kingfisher swoops.

That summer we fell in love.
The leaves and burrs reduced
to humus. Worms
worked the soil, and were pulled by blackbirds.
Weather from the mid-Atlantic
no longer creaked the boughs
that overlooked the fields,
the house, the tennis courts,
the woman milking cows
in 1895, or us, the lovers who
of all the generations
heard it, without axe or lightning, fall.
For months we burned oak wood,
centuries of heat and light.

A Ritual to Read to Each Other   William Stafford

If you don't know the kind of person I am
and I don't know the kind of person you are
a pattern that others made may prevail in the world
and following the wrong god home we may miss our star.

For there is many a small betrayal in the mind,
a shrug that lets the fragile sequence break
sending with shouts the horrible errors of childhood
storming out to play through the broken dyke.

And as elephants parade holding each elephant's tail,
but if one wanders the circus won't find the park,
I call it cruel and maybe the root of all cruelty
to know what occurs but not recognise the fact.

And so I appeal to a voice, to something shadowy,
a remote important region in all who talk:
though we could fool each other, we should consider –
lest the parade of our mutual life get lost in the dark.

For it is important that awake people be awake,
or a breaking line may discourage them back to sleep;
the signals we give – yes or no, or maybe – should be clear:
the darkness around us is deep.

When the Hunger is Here
and the Anger

Em Strang

When the hunger is here and the anger,
the horses lift their muzzles and snort
in the manner of horses, truthfully,
with a mane-flicking, hoof-stomping truth
that sticks to the roof of your mouth
as you watch from the edge of the field,
floodwater lapping a hollow
where the grass slowly sinks;
as though the water were the night drawing down
or the closing curtains of a time
when fine brown horses canter
to the edge of the fabric,
waiting for you to find your voice and raise it,
waiting for you to take the reins
when the hunger is here and the anger.

When the hunger is here and the anger,
you remember the rich man
who starved his horses,
how they died painfully, slowly,
over weeks of neglect and mistreatment,

how their ribs stopped their skin
from sinking deeper,
how their eyes stopped breathing on the final day
– brown beadlet anemones with no sea –
how he never knew the coarse brown coat of the mare
nor the way the stallion hoofed the fence to be with her,
knowing the only way to live is with others,
whether they're hurting or dancing or dying,
no matter how hard it rains or how deep the fields fill
when the hunger is here and the anger.

When the hunger is here and the anger,
there's no room for the necessity of grief
and the small bird of the body
stabs its beak into the day again and again,
like a robot working a conveyor belt;
and all sense of faith is lost in an endless flight
from the soft feathers of the self,
from the bird's precise, miraculous migration
from one timeless, embodied life to another,
covering thousands of miles without stopping
to look back, without suffering the hooks of doubt or lack,
as though the path is clear for every small bird, every swallow
and bunting, every finch who lands at the new lake
and drinks the brown floodwater gratefully, with relief,
when the hunger is here and the anger.

When the hunger is here and the anger
and the path is littered with clear-fell and bombed homes
and burnt-out faces of people broken
in the way the racehorse is broken,
hurdle after hurdle,
sweat steaming off it like a ghost-horse,
one after the other withering into a grey sky,
all of us racehorses with anemone eyes,
stinging and seeking
with blind hands and blind feet –
then you know that the song the small birds sing
is the one you belong to,
the song you and everyone else
can bring into the long dark days
when the hunger is here and the anger.

No Nature Poems, Please

Rob Lewis

It seemed an odd request for a poetry magazine. I don't even remember the name of it. It was one of many thousands with listings in the 1994 *Poet's Market*, a compendium of poetry journals and their submission guidelines. There at the end of its blurb, italicised for emphasis, was the strange plea – *no nature poems, please.*

If it was just the one publication, I might not have noticed. But as I leafed through the pages I saw it again and again, always at the end of the blurb, always italicised for emphasis – *no nature poems, please.* I didn't quite know what to make of it. Was this merely a device to turn away a kind of stereotype, the rhyming ode to butterflies and sunshine? Would a pared down, mytho-poetic take on bear scat, à la Gary Snyder, be acceptable? Was the nature poem merely falling out of fashion, or was something more profound going on?

What stuck with me most, though, was the very notion of a 'nature poem'. What is such a thing? How, in this age, do you define it? How were these editors defining it?

We have a general idea about the nature poem. It is something with a long tradition. It is about a 'nature' that is out there, around us, but not necessarily inside us or interacting with us. It often bears the feeling of adulation, with the poet cast as a small thing before a large and powerful apparition.

But in the present age, with a sixth great extinction underway and the climate wrecking-ball swinging through time toward pretty much everything alive, does the nature poem as we commonly think of it still exist? And by extension, does the received tradition still sing true? Maybe those editors heard a dissonance, an unnaturalness, that's worth taking note of.

Of course, to define the nature poem you first must define 'nature'. For me that's pretty simple. Nature is *all*. It is space and time and all the relationships and particulars between, which includes stars and sand grains, songbirds and air, photosynthesis and respiration, frogs and gravity and cedars and, of course, us. After all, we share 70% of our DNA with sea sponges. The reason we test our poisons on rats and mice is because we share the same ancient evolutionary pathway. And of course we all wear the vestiges of tails in our tail bones.

This notion, of the human physically emerging from nature, is nothing new. Science accepts and explains it as evolution. We can take it one step further, though, to say that our inner qualities, like those of spirit and creativity, also derive from nature. We sing love songs because love and singing are inherent in nature. We write poems and paint canvasses because self-expression is inherent in nature. What is a flower doing but expressing itself?

With this rounder, more inclusive view of nature, the notion of a separate category of poem called the nature poem becomes a little problematic. If there is to be a special category, perhaps it should be the non-nature poem. We could call it the anthro-poem. But again, where would you find such a thing? That is, how and where do you end nature?

A few weeks after my encounter with *Poet's Market*, I was on a Greyhound bus on my way to Denver. It was night. Our darkened tunnel with its hooded aisle lights raced through an even darker tunnel of highway. I looked around at the tilting, bobbing heads and thought, 'I could write it now' – the non-nature poem, that is. There we were, humans only, encapsulated in a machine, the world out our windows hidden by night, indecipherable. No nature in there, right? But someone must have had an apple in their bag, which was filling the cabin with the sweet tang of an apple orchard. And there was the watery chorus of our own breathing, and with it the watery reminder of our breathing intimacy with plants. Our craft was built with steel hacked from mountains, fuelled by the compressed and composted residue of ancient life layered on ancient life. Our wheels were round, the signature shape of nature.

And we were rolling on a planet rolling toward the sun. Out my window a thin line of red appeared on the horizon, as if the horizon had been slit and risen with blood. Milky pools of mist hung in the folds of pasture. The bus banked a long curve and through the shoulders of two hills a shaft of light found a chestnut mare standing alone in a field, igniting in the haze around her a rainbow halo of refracted luminescence.

Involuntarily, I gasped, and then looked down the rows to see if anyone heard, but everyone was asleep. I wanted to nudge the person ahead of me and tap the glass, saying 'Hurry, look.' Instead I gathered pen and journal and followed an instinct familiar to poets, to record the sublime indication, the brief revelation, to not let such magic be lost to a world literally racing by. And then I laughed to myself; writing a nature poem again.

When the bus arrived in Denver I had a couple hours to kill waiting for my ride, so I wandered over to Tattered Cover Books, Denver's largest bookstore, and found the poetry section in the magazine racks. I was curious to see how *no nature poems, please* was playing out there.

As for nature, human and non-human, things were not looking so good. The forces of economic globalism were being loosed on the earth. Capital roamed the globe with digital ease and at fibre optic speed. Small farming communities were collapsing around the world. The mining of the oceans and gang rape of primeval forests proceeded apace with corporate efficiency. And Bill McKibben's once lonely cry about climate change, first uttered in 1988 with the publication of *The End of Nature*, was being echoed by a loudening chorus of very alarmed scientists of every imaginable discipline.

Botanists saw plants blossoming strangely early, lepidopterists saw butterfly larvae starving as a result, oceanographers saw the chemistry of the oceans turning acidic, hydrologists saw glaciers withdrawing, herpetologists saw frogs disappearing almost overnight. So I was naturally curious about what poetry was seeing. What did poetry have to say about this broad-scale calamity befalling the earth? I picked up one journal then another, scanning the contents, looking for clues. Gradually, I realised, at least according to my little sample, the answer was nothing, nothing at all.

These were publications popular enough to earn a place in the racks of Denver's largest bookstore, and included such stalwarts as the *Paris Review* and *Poetry*. Like *Poet's Market*, they arrived via the marketing of poetry, the business end of the stick, and as such I felt they represented poetry in an 'official' sort of way. If we can speak of a poetry establishment, the publications before me were its product.

Hearing echoes of *no nature poems, please*, I put the last quarterly back on the rack and stood there feeling strangely dislocated, and perhaps a little ashamed. 'Who am I, some sort of poetry cop? Why not let people write whatever they want?' This was not a role I relished, yet I felt I had stumbled onto something. Or more accurately, I felt I had stumbled upon a fairly significant *absence* of something, a silence where there should have been a clamour.

A couple of racks over, toward the back of the store, I noticed some magazines I recognised and walked over. It was the environmental section. Here was the earth in all her haemorrhaging. We all know the litany, and I can't say it was easy reading. I found it data-heavy, too prone to viewing nature through the lens of science. What would happen, I wondered, if they looked through a poetic lens? What would that read like? I looked back over at the poetry stacks. Ten short paces away, yet a separate world. How did this happen?

Was this split due somehow to the very growth and success of 'environmentalism'? That is, was a kind of language and cultural split happening? Branching one way went the science-loving vernacular and politically engaged culture of environmentalism. Branching off in a different direction went the science-wary language and politically aloof culture of poetry.

Then I looked over and saw a cluster of magazines about woodworking, another about computers. There was an especially long section on cars and hot rods, but also a place for knitters, bass fishers and body builders, etc.

How odd it seemed. All these varied categories of human interest, each depending on the same invisible: nature. Without nature no wood to work, no wool to knit, no bass to catch, no body to build. And yet the awareness of and concern for this nature was concentrated and divided off into a tiny section near the back of the store. You may need nature, may breathe and be nature, but unless your individual identity includes 'environmentalist' you're not likely to fight for it, let alone visit the little rack at the back of the store.

Our notion of wilderness is marked by an absence of fences. Wilderness begins where the fences end. And where wilderness ends is where the fences begin again, where the land becomes demarcated and divided, contained and tamed. What we don't realise is this same thing is happening inside us. Perhaps within the human personality there once ranged something akin to wilderness, undefined by interests and ideologies, and perhaps there are places (indigenous communities, for instance) where that sort of personality still thrives. But in modern society we are as mapped and subdivided as the cities around us. When the editor stipulated *no nature poems, please*, who was stipulating what?

*

As time went on I noticed that *no nature poems, please* disappeared as a submission guideline from *Poet's Market*. Perhaps some people like me complained. I continued to peruse the poetry stacks of the local magazine store. A friend gave me a subscription to *Poets &*

Writers, a hefty bi-monthly with contest announcements and calls for submissions, notices for grants and awards, residencies and retreats, writer interviews, essays on craft, and lots of advertisements for the burgeoning MFA in Poetry industry. I also attended readings and went to the occasional poetry conference. Like this, I continued my very unscientific and purely observational research on the relations and interactions between poetry and the worsening condition of more-than-human nature.

Eventually, the plight of nature did seem to penetrate the editorial scaffold of the poetry establishment, though in a rather academic way. I began noticing MFA programs offerings special disciplines in things like 'eco-poetics' and 'environmental literature'. The intention made sense, but I knew it would lead to yet more categorisation and division, more demarcation. As for a spirited defence of nature by poetry at large, I've yet to detect one.

Writer and translator Robert Bly describes just such a defence in his book *News of The Universe: Poems of Twofold Consciousness*. In Europe, in the late 1700s and into the mid-1800s, the Cartesian split was spreading, with an increasingly analytical and utilitarian view of nature sweeping through the culture. Poets like William Blake, Novalis, Gerard De Nerval and Goethe fought back.

> Free thinker! Do you think you are the only thinker
> on this earth in which life blazes inside all things?
> Your liberty does what it wishes with the power it controls,
> but when you gather to plan, the universe is not there.
> – Gerard De Nerval, 1854

This movement has been lumped in with Romanticism, but Bly saw something more combative there. Bly saw poets agitating to defend the very divinity and integrity of nature, which was being systematically undermined by a system of rationality that Goethe described as 'grey, monstrous and death-like [...] as if facing a ghost.'

Is it time for a similar front now? Is it time for the warrior poet?

As for the present model, where science is the medium and scientific language the vernacular, the gap between nature and society is only widening. Indeed, like so much else these days, the model itself seems to be approaching collapse.

'And then we wept.'
    – Professor Terry Hughes, head of the ARC Centre for Excellence
    for Coral Reef Studies at James Cook University.

When Professor Hughes apprised his students of the results of his recent aerial surveys of the Great Barrier Reef, there was nothing for them to do but weep. The research showed the reef was clearly dying, becoming a white ghost under the strangely warm waters.

Science is supposed to be impassive about its subject. So when marine biologists come to tears over their data, you could say the scientific method, and the language it uses, is brushing up against its own limits. For where do you go from there? Launch another study? Gather more data?

I suspect this isn't an isolated event. There is likely much private weeping amongst scientists confronting incomprehensible loss while expected to maintain an air of cool objectivity. In his film *How to Let Go of the World and Love Everything Climate Can't Change*, Josh Fox interviews a number of leading experts about the harrowing realities surrounding climate collapse and related extinction. They include Michael Mann, whose climate research led to the infamous 'hockey stick' graph; Lester Brown, founder of the Earth Policy Institute; and Elizabeth Kolbert, author of *The Sixth Great Extinction: An Unnatural History*. The most telling part of the interviews isn't in the information these experts convey, but in the silence each one eventually trails off into, eyes looking away or down, as though at an abyss.

It is a heart-gripping silence, and their faces tell a story their data can't. What can speak into such a silence? What can bring meaning to it and offer pathways not for the analysing intellect, but the suffering soul? When science is struck dumb, who picks up the narrative?

I think humans have always needed some sort of intermediary, a medium say, between the human and non-human. In ancient times, and still in indigenous cultures, that medium was a shamanic figure and, more loosely, the medium consisted of stories and rituals which regularly renewed the flow of regard and reciprocation between human and non-human. Eventually civilisation appointed science as the medium. But, as we see, science – like the earth – has limits.

*

Is the answer to *no nature poems, please* more nature poems, please? I don't think so. That's too simplistic, and it still leaves us with the false category of the 'nature poem'. I think it's something more like this – tear down the walls, break up the categories, open the channels. Allow poetry to flow into science, science into prayer, prayer into nature, nature into poetry, and around and around let it go. Interpenetration is in the nature of things. We could use some now amongst the ranks of disciplines which clamour to explain the world to us: science, environmentalism, politics, psychology, religion etc.

It would be nice for us to all breathe the same air for once, not different versions of it – the scientist's version, a combination of gasses; the environmentalist's version, a combination of gasses requiring protection and regulation; the politician's version, something the 'environmental voter' cares about; the psychologist's version, something which when breathed properly can help reduce anxiety; the religious version, something God gave us (presumably to poison and corrupt?); the poet's version – ah, here is where it gets interesting.

In his essay 'Nature', Ralph Waldo Emerson describes walking down a country lane outside Boston amongst twenty or thirty farms. 'Miller owns this field, Locke that, and Manning the woodland beyond. But none of them owns the landscape.' There is only one, he says, 'whose eye can integrate all the parts, that is, the poet.' The poet, beholden to no particular category, is the natural integrator and, by the same logic, the natural barrier breaker. Perhaps this is why poetry seems to resist environmentalism. It doesn't want to own one farm or another. It wants the freedom to own the whole landscape. How strange that this freedom now makes it indispensable to the very institutions it tries to avoid.

Society needs the poet right now. It is an age of irony and reversals and this is one of them. If we have forgotten what air is, have lost sight of its divine formula – plant and animal breathing life into each other – who but the poet to remind us? If we have lost our enchantment with nature, who but the poet to re-enchant us, to retune our senses to nature's hidden energies and mysteries? For every scientific explanation of nature, there is a poetic explanation. And it's the poetic explanation the human narrative now requires.

The practice of poetry brings certain standards: a deeper intensity of observation, the freedom to see the sacred anywhere and everywhere, the courage of heart-seeing, the determination to make words meet their subjects with fidelity and power. Useful qualities for a craft that tries so assiduously not to be useful.

But it's not just human society that needs the poet, it's societies of birds and reptiles, forests and coral reefs. Nature, slowly collapsing into silence, calls out louder than ever for the poet. Now we all need what the poet brings: the broken-open hearts of words, the wild articulation, the howl.

Seven Circles in *The Book of Sharks*   Rob Carney

The cousin of a shark is a manta ray;
and the cousin of a manta ray, a hawk;

and the cousin of a hawk is lightning, the ocean reborn,
returned skyward and alive with storm;

and the cousin of storms is a waterfall;
and the cousin of falling is the wind;

and the cousin of wind is erosion
leaving rock, the bones of the mountains, scattered;

and the cousin of the mountains is a row of teeth,
and another, and another behind;

and those teeth are the cousin of the manta ray,
lightning, the wind …

*

In a story seldom remembered, sharks were ghosts
guarding the afterlife

since their rendered bodies had no skeletons,
just teeth.

The shock of that discovery
must have added new verses to songs

and widened the net of old omens,
but nobody knows. Those details

aren't the details that lasted.
Only this: The dead

step out of their bodies, walk down
to the sea, swim out to the horizon.

For some, the passage is easy –
a day, a night, a warm current there to guide them.

For others, the journey goes on and on –
if they killed a bear, or left a wolf's mate howling –

and the water is cold as a shark's eyes.
And then they see the fins.

Under the first full moon of summer,
they would carry bowls of water,

the light reflected on the surface making more,
a procession of moons moving forward.

In the centre of town was a rowboat
being filled one bowl at a time,

and this was the boat of anyone lost at sea,
gone without a burial.

Those in mourning floated candles and petals.
There may have been music on flute or strings,

but we don't know; it's a ritual fallen away,
and all we have left are the wives' tales.

They say their empty bowls filled with quieter sorrow,
and with memories of the dead to carry home.

They say the boat would be gone come sunrise,
just the anchor there,

still as a headstone
by others from the years before.

*

We have one such anchor on display in the museum,
arrangements of fishhooks,

even spears tipped long ago with sharks' teeth,
and figure, *That's that,*

think the past
fits into our pockets.

We wander about
then buy a bar-code souvenir.

But the past is more like the wind behind us,
and the present more like a ship,

and the only pockets on a ship that matter
are the sails ...

*

and they're wrong about the skeletons,
apart from the age of the bones,

bones buried deep but seated upright together,
all of them facing the sea –

so the ancient world believed in guardian spirits
watching over the living,

and a salmon was placed with the deceased
to keep the spirit fed.

Fish bones wrapped in deerskin
were discovered in every grave –

a plausible explanation, but it's wrong.
The living were playing the part of angels,

guiding the dead to the edge of heaven,
seating them upright to find Forever in the waves.

But what about the salmon?
Well, that's counterclockwise too:

The salmon were meant as an offering,
a present for the sharks,

a thank-you for taking our spirits
into their home.

*

Spearing a shark means seven days of work –
that long to do the rendering –

and all you get is a set of jaws and teeth,
some fragment to hang in a window

or look at over the fireplace
instead of at the fire.

I've heard there are monks somewhere
using human skulls as paperweights.

Not to keep old scrolls from rolling up,
or pages in place while they bind them,

but to bear in mind
we aren't the measure of Creation. Just a part.

*

The edge of the sea is a teacher –
so many bones:

all the shells and the sand dollars,
all the barnacles encrusted on the pier,

even wood –
it used to stand upright in forests –

even ash left behind in our fire pits
dug to keep warm, to boil water

and empty our crab pots ...
even steam rising up like the spirit of rivers,

joining clouds that drift above our graveyards,
and higher still

the moon keeps sailing through its phases,
all of them the colour of bone.

Earth Day 2012   Catherine Owen

There is everything now, at nearly the end of April, or almost everything,
    out of the all   we have left: crows &

    geese, ladybugs & spiders, Indian plum

& cherry blossom & now the swallows
    return, a tan-blue zag of them over
        the river, speeding up the air towards summer, their wings,

as they cursive around me, are pleating with light – their beaks slide into
                drainpipes,
    their bodies slip within stucco holes where the small cargo of nests

waits.

As if I had not imagined anything like this
    before – the earth given back to itself each year, generous

    despite our lessenings

       & the machines almost prostrate themselves before this power

that has nothing to do with forgiveness, that hushes grief.

The Owl in the Mask of the Dreamer   John Haines

Nothing bestial or human remains
in all the brass and tin
that we strike and break and weld.

Nothing of the hand-warmed stone
made flesh, of the poured heat
filling breast, belly, and thigh.

The craft of an old affection
that called by name the lion shape
of night, gave rain its body

and the wind its mouth – the owl
in the mask of the dreamer,
one of the animal stones asleep ...

By tinker and by cutting torch
reduced to a fist of slag,
to a knot of rust on a face of chrome.

So, black dust of the grinding wheels,
bright and sinewy curl of metal
fallen beneath the lathe:

Speak for these people of drawn wire
striding towards each other
over a swept square of bronze.

For them the silence is loud
and the sunlight is strong.

No matter how far they walk
they will never be closer.

The Inverness Almanac
Nina Pick in Conversation with Cate Chapman

The Inverness Almanac is
a semi-annual print publication project;
a record and an artifact for posterity;
a collection of practical knowledge
and rumination about our natural world;
an outlet for creative expression.

The Inverness Almanac is
a reflection of this confluence of place, time and community.
an expression of the desire for connection,
and for deep knowing of the interdependence of everything.

The Inverness Almanac is
in honor of our ancestors,
and in service to the great mystery of here, now.

*

CC: You're one fifth of the core editorial team working on the *Inverness Almanac*; how would you describe the project?

NP: The *Inverness Almanac* is a bi-annual softback publication, containing a mixture of prose, poetry, visual art and work that isn't easily categorised. As a project it's very place based, relating specifically to our community and landscape here in Inverness, which is in Marin County, Northern California. It's about the nature of intimate relationship with place in the broadest sense of the word: spiritual relationship, physical relationship and community.

Inverness is a small town which is part of Point Reyes National Seashore. It's an incredibly special, sacred place right on Tomales Bay. It is like a small village which preserves elements of traditional community which are very difficult to find in the US. There is something about Inverness in particular: this is, in a way, a somewhat mystical location which is part of this incredible wider landscape of Point Reyes. It's a place that offers and holds something that is really lost in American culture, both in terms of the landscape and in terms of the culture, the community, the creativity. There is something about the way people live, which is I think slower and more creative and more connected than most other towns that I've experienced in the US. So it's holding something that we try to offer in what we share from this place: a way of sharing a vision of what relationship with place can look like in a way that really honours the earth, honours community, honours spirit.

cc: You've spoken about the desire to share something about your community and the place you live in; were there any other drivers/aspirations/concerns that brought the project into being? Is there something in the context of how unusual this sort of deeply rooted community feels now, and how perhaps that might not have been so unusual, say, 150 years ago?

np: Yes, that's exactly it. It's a vision of not only a nostalgic way of being (which it is for sure, and I think that's partly what resonates with our readership), but for me it's also a vision of what we're working towards, what a potentiality there is. And the other inspiration is that there's a really high creative concentration in this community and a connection with nature which is very much lost in our highly technological, rapid-paced society. The people here are really tuned in: they know the tides; they know when there's bioluminescence in the bay; they know where the moon is in its cycle; where to plant at different times. And this sense of place feels pretty unique right now, so there is knowledge there and a way of being that it's important to share.

CC: So to share, and I guess to propagate, in a way?

NP: Yes, absolutely. And it's been interesting because a lot of our readership has come from places that we didn't expect: San Francisco, LA... people have bought it from all over the country. And I think it's because it holds something that's so lost and that we really have a longing for, which is exactly that intimacy with place. What is it to be in intimate, sensual, tactile relationship with land? And I think we – all of us – have a profound desire for that.

CC: There is an intimate relationship between community and place and for me the *Almanac* recognises and explores this, bringing together disparate experiences of West Marin to create a collective voice. How do you feel the publications have affected the community of contributors, both in terms of their relationship with West Marin and with each other?

NP: I would say that's been a big aspect of our enterprise: being a community endeavour. Not only in terms of the publication, but in terms of events that we've hosted. We've had a really beautiful event – a poetry reading – in Point Reyes National Seashore, in the park, with Robert Hass and a young poet about to publish his first book, David Bailey. They read together: a young poet and a really well-established poet, both local and both of whose work is really inspired by their relationship to this place. And the reading was outside, no mics. It was beautiful, in this natural amphitheatre. We've also had a large music event, and release parties where we've had poetry readings, bands play, dancing, DJs... it's a way of bringing together this really diverse community.

One aspect of this community is that it's made up primarily of older people – there's not a lot of youthful creative output because it's

43

a difficult place to find jobs. The young people are being perpetually displaced from their homes as the rentals are being put on places like Airbnb and are no longer affordable for young people. So it was also important to have representation of the youth in this community; the youngest contributor we had in our last issue was five years old and we've also had writing from a teenager who's an old student of mine, and our oldest contributor (I think!) is in their seventies. So it's important to us to have a range of voices from the community, from children and adolescents through to elders, and also to have events that can appeal to the range of the community. We also want to ignite and spark from a place of youthful energy and see what that can bring to the community in terms of a life force which has been somewhat dampened in recent years due to the financial and economic situation.

cc: So do you feel that the *Almanac* has created connections, and particularly intergenerational connections, that wouldn't have been there otherwise?

NP: Oh, definitely. Without a doubt. Our events are amazing, they make my heart wide open: we're gathered in this small space – people from all sections of the community, young and old – and we've really tried to hold space for that kind of diversity. There is definitely more we can do too. There's a big Latino community in Point Reyes and Inverness which isn't that well represented in general and one thing I want to do (and that we haven't quite succeeded in yet) is to have pieces that are both in Spanish and translated to have diversity in that aspect as well.

cc: So the *Almanac* has created connections within the community of contributors; do you feel it has also affected their sense of place?

NP: That has really been the goal and I really do hope so. One key element of the *Almanac* is the visual tide chart which runs along the bottom of each page, coupled with a range of data relating to seasonal flora and fauna. I think in providing this, what we're really trying to offer is a moment of meditation: like, 'Oh, today is April 27th. What's going on with the tide? What's going on with the moon? What can I look out for while I'm going on my hike?' It's a contemplative space that we're hoping to foster. And I think there's something special about that relationship between what is going on in the page in terms of the data or the tide chart at the bottom, and the poem or the artwork that's on the page above it; providing a physical space for contemplation, for reflection, that will hopefully draw the reader into greater intimacy in their natural landscape – wherever they may be – and with themselves and their own contemplative life.

CC: What impact has the *Almanac* had in the wider community, beyond the community of contributors?

NP: One goal that we have in terms of the events that we put on is to open up poetry and literature to wider audiences in ways that are radical, non-traditional and enlivening. I think that's a huge driving force for us: we don't want to have some stuffy event with wine and cheese at two in the afternoon on a Sunday in the library. I think what we're all driven by is radical energy, maybe even anarchic energy. And I see the radical potential of poetry, and I want to be working from that edge, all the time.

CC: You've said that some of your readership, surprisingly, is in very urban areas – is there a difference in the feedback you're getting from there in contrast with the local community, or do you feel that these are really universal themes that are speaking to everybody in similar ways?

NP: It's a great question. A lot of our copies move through Point Reyes Books (which is a fabulous independent bookstore) and these are sold not just to locals but also to a huge number of tourists, as Point Reyes is a very large tourist destination. One thing that (we hope!) is happening is that the *Almanac* helps people who are visiting the area to really deepen their relationship with the place, so that they're coming not only as consumers. I think that this is the danger in tourism:

45

that you come for the day and you *take*. You take pictures, you get as much from the experience as you can and it's not reciprocal. You're not sitting with the land, in a mutual relationship with it. For me that's somewhat missing the point of what it means to be in relationship, so the hope is that the *Almanac* can disseminate a way of being in relationship with wildness that can help someone visiting the area more truly meet that need inside themselves and to more truly be in reciprocity with the local land and community.

In terms of our urban readership, the places where we're stocked and where we move a lot of copies are these hip boutiques. I feel like we're the anti-hip; I don't get it at all! Because one of our major goals is timelessness, earnestness... we're like, 'Screw irony!' We want it to be from the heart, heartfelt. That for me is the primary goal, that facing into reality. The opposite of hipster culture: so vapid, so empty, all virtual, all screens, nothing real. We want to move beyond that veil, beyond that image to say, 'This is real life! Cold water, solid ground.' I think that approach is very refreshing and something that we feel at a soul level and that isn't being met by our culture on a wider scale. So I think when someone in, say, San Francisco, finds a copy of this in some boutique, what I imagine is happening (and I'm not really sure) is that something on an unconscious level, some unconscious yearning, is being met. That's my suspicion. And it might be something that isn't even languageable. Having lived in urban areas myself I know how that longing goes underground when it isn't being met – that longing to see the night sky, to see the stars, being able to hear birds. For me it's a kind of soul death when that need isn't being met, and there are layers of numbness that build up. So if there's anything we can do to break through to that deep wellspring, that's really important work.

CC: Do you see fertile ground in the relationship between the *Dark Mountain Project* and the *Inverness Almanac*? For me there are deep parallels, with this particular difference of the *Almanac* being very

46

place-based, whereas *Dark Mountain* doesn't so much have that specificity – other than (hopefully!) bringing you back to the place where you, the reader, are. The two projects seem so interrelated.

NP: Yeah, I really see that and one thing that I've been inspired by in terms of the *Dark Mountain Project* is the sense of that international community. And it's something that we've started to move in the direction of, partly because our local community is so small. We've started opening up our call for submissions to a wider audience in terms of staying with the themes of intimacy with place but having a more wide-ranging pool of contributors, and I see that as something that *Dark Mountain* does brilliantly. And I love reading the work, receiving the anthology – I'm in Inverness and I'm receiving this anthology from the UK and I'm like, 'Yes! This is exactly what's going on!' There's this sense of resonance that transcends place, boundary, language. It's a real sense that, 'Okay! Someone's finally speaking my language!' Because we're really at the margins of a culture.

On our office wall we have the *Dark Mountain Manifesto* which is a huge motivation for me as a writer. I love that idea of writing 'with dirt under my fingernails' – it's my measure of success as a poet – I'm like, 'Okay, how dirty is this? How in the earth is that writing?' So I'd say that's a huge inspiration for what we publish. We want these rougher edges. We want work that's rolling around in the mud, that just went skinny dipping in Tomales Bay at midnight…

CC: How has your vision of the *Almanac* changed since the first publication in spring/summer 2015? How has the project evolved through the dialogue between contributors and the editorial team?

NP: At the beginning it was envisioned as a strictly local publication, where all the contributors would come from a fairly limited area of Point Reyes, West Marin, Coastal Marin. What we found by our third issue was that we had to start opening it out because that's a pretty small pool, and also because our readership had expanded and we had started to receive submissions from further away. So I think if someone sent us something that resonated with the deeper themes of our projects and was a dynamic piece of writing or art, then we would include it for sure, because we're now less driven by strictly geographical limitations and more by thematic goals or the life of the *Almanac* itself, it feels like it's kind of become its own being. So we're asking, 'What does it want to become?' I think that's been the big question or motivation for each issue.

In terms of where the *Almanac* is situated in our wider trajectory as editors/publishers, it's a project that we've been involved in for a number of years and we're now moving into publishing in a larger way as Mount Vision Press. We're about to publish our first book of poetry in September and this is the kind of work we want to be publishing: to be pushing the edges of what literature can do; we might move into music as well, and there are musicians within the editorial team. One of the team has recorded a number of albums which are really an aural representation of what Inverness sounds like; we want to do a podcast, an audio almanac with sounds of this space, poetry and music, as well as recordings of – for example – what's happening on top of Mount Vision, on Marshall Beach etc.

CC: When you put the first issue together did you have a sense of what media you wanted to include? Have you always had a broad vision of what you wanted to include in terms of written and visual work, or has this evolved with the *Almanac*?

NP: That's been our vision from the beginning: to expand on the idea of what text is. For example, we have a musical transcription of birdsong. So what is that? Is it a piece of music? Is it a transcription? Is it poetry? Art? And that's been something that we've hoped to draw in by expanding our pool of contributors, to move more into this vision we've had since the beginning and to manifest that more in reality, pushing up against the edges of what counts as literary or artistic work. It makes me think of *The Spell of the Sensuous* by David Abram. How does language itself emerge out of nature? How can we

48

read it, interpret it? And you'll see in the last issue (Volume 3) that we have some beautiful photographs by one of the editors, Katie Eberle, of just... sand. And this is about the way that nature is itself art, is creating art, and is poetry, is creating poetry. So I think we want to keep on pushing that and see where it can go.

CC: What are your plans for ongoing engagement with the themes explored in the *Almanac*? Do you envision the project spreading out to other communities/locations? Or is it more about deepening into your local community via events and media other than the *Almanac* itself? (How) do you see it disseminating?

NP: Yeah, a number of people have said to me, 'Oh, I'd love to have an almanac in my community.' I don't see us expanding the model, but I hope that it would be an inspiration for other people to do that in their own way, drawing on what is unique in their community and their land. For our own team, we're currently working on our fourth issue which will come out this fall and at the same time we're publishing our first poetry book and I see this as a part of our expansion – expanding in genre, coming up against the growing edge of what our creative work is as a group. There are five of us as editors, so what is this particular alchemy? What is wanting to come into form in the kind of magic that is the five of us? So after this fourth issue we're not going to be publishing another *Almanac*, at least for the time being. And if we do indeed publish another issue we might change the form of it to maybe doing an *Almanac* that's the whole year; one of our goals is continual reinvention, continually being at our creative edge and our creative potential. So I think that's partially why we're moving from the *Almanac* to creating the poetry book to whatever's next. We would love to create and publish a book of photographs, we want to press some records... there's a whole list! We don't want to be in that easy resting place of having it down, knowing how it works, of things being predictable. We want to see how we can keep on pushing that edge.

CC: How has the *Almanac* altered or developed your own relationship with your home? Has drawing that perspective from many other contributors materially altered the way that you experience where you are and your community?

NP: It really has. I'm originally from Massachusetts, from the East Coast, so this is not my native land. In the first issue I have an essay about moving to the area, because it was a profound experience for me. It was very unfamiliar and somewhat uncanny, going from the East Coast – where everything is known, small, really pretty miniature in scale – to this wild California. I'd lived in California for a number of years in more urban areas before I moved out here, and all of a sudden there was this explosion of life force in myself that was like a reflection of what it was to be living in this landscape. It felt like a peeling away of the extra layers of myself, coming into something more core. And my writing dramatically shifted; I felt what it was to be a writer in this place. My work changed. I felt both the wildness of the place and the safety of this community – because I really let my guard down and was held in a way that I hadn't felt in urban areas, knowing people. So I'd say that my work as a writer led me really down and really deep, and at the end of that process became much more infused with light. Because the light in this place is really … you just see it in people's artwork and people's writing across the board, because it's like its own living breathing alive thing, and it's pro-found. Looking back at the evolution of my own work I saw how that transformation took place. And I learned a lot about the natural landscape here, which (not growing up here) was unfamiliar to me.

A lot of the young people come from other places. One of our other editors, however, has lived his whole life in this area and has a deeper understanding of the wildlife and the land than any person

[opposite] KATE EBERLE *Limantour I* (detail)
Photograph of Limantour Beach, Point Reyes, California.

51

I've ever met, and so he brings that profound relationship. In fact the whole aesthetic of the *Almanac* reflects the fact that he speaks 'Inverness' as a native language. So we're a combination of both looking at this place from the outside and coming in to it, and looking at it from many many years of deeply inhabiting it. And that's the kind of alchemy of the five of us, that each of us is coming from a different perspective.

CC: You've spoken about the radical potential of writing, and specifically of poetry. Why do you see that as important in the context of the converging crises of our time? Why do we need that?

NP: I think it's absolutely crucial. We've lost the power of metaphor. You can see it in American politics at the moment for example; there's a deficit of imagination, of the imaginal life, of myth. And metaphor is sacred; this is one way, I think, of understanding spirit. I mean, we can't name it, right? It's ineffable. But we can have myth, we can have metaphor that helps us experience it in an embodied way. I think that's what a good poem is doing, it's circumambulating the epicentre.

Our culture and our politics – and I'm speaking about the US – are made up of these levels of superficiality. We have this highly technological society that for all its connectivity is highly disconnected, and I think in that same way there's also a sense of the highly literal and a loss of the value of mythic relationship, and without that level of myth and of metaphor I think we start to get lost as a culture – losing the storytelling around the fire, for example. We need myth and we need metaphor on a deep soul level, and poetry brings that.

CC: And what is the place of poetry in working towards the goals you've spoken about for the *Almanac*?

NP: I think it's the absolute essence. I think that poetry offers what other forms of creative work attempt, in a way that is... well, it's beyond language. Poetry circles around the epicentre; it gets really really *really* close to the unlanguageable and opens it up for maybe a brief second – you get to the end of the poem and there's that amazing brutal twist that happens in a good piece of poetry. And then maybe, just for a second, you glimpse it: the mystery, the ineffable. And so there's something incredibly divine in that, and incredibly radical. So that's my goal as an editor, that's my dream around the submissions that we publish: to include work that just cracks wide open. Of course not everything does that, but I want to be moving in the direction of that goal. And I think poetry, in its potentiality, does that unlike any other creative form. So what is the goal of poetry? It's circling around the unnameable thing. It doesn't necessarily succeed in naming it at all, but it's about that attempt.

En vinternatt

Stormen sätter sin mun till huset
och blåser för att få ton.
Jag sover oroligt, vänder mig, läser
blundande stormens text.

Men barnets ögon är stora i mörkret
och stormen den gnyr för barnet.
Båda tycker om lampor som svänger.
båda är halvvägs mot språket.

Stormen har barnsliga händer och vingar.
Karavanen skenar mot Lappland.
Och huset känner sin stjärnbild av spikar
som håller väggarna samman.

Natten är stilla över vårt golv.
(där alla förklingade steg
vilar som sjunkna löv i en damm)
men därute är natten vild!

A Winter Night

Tomas Tranströmer
(Trans. Robert Bly)

The storm puts its lips to the house
    and blows to make a sound.
I sleep restlessly, turn over, with closed
    eyes read the book of the storm.

But the child's eyes grow huge in the dark
    and the storm whimpers for the child.
Both love to see the swinging lamp.
    Both are halfway toward speech.

Storms have childlike hands and wings.
    The caravan bolts off towards Lapland
and the house senses the constellation of nails
    holding its walls together.

The night is quiet above our floor
    (where all the died-away footsteps
are lying like sunken leaves in a pond)
    but outside the night is wild!

Över världen går en mer allvarlig storm.
   Den sätter sin mun till vår själ
och blåser för att få ton. Vi räds
   att stormen blåser oss tomma.

A more serious storm is moving over us all.
　　It puts its lips to our soul
and blows to make a sound. We're afraid
　　　the storm will blow everything inside us away.

The Beauty of Things

Robinson Jeffers

To feel and speak the astonishing beauty of things –
    earth, stone and water,
Beast, man and woman, sun, moon and stars –
The blood-shot beauty of human nature, its thoughts,
    frenzies and passions.
And unhuman nature its towering reality –
For man's half dream; man, you might say,
    is nature dreaming, but rock
And water and sky are constant – to feel
Greatly, and understand greatly, and express greatly, the natural
Beauty, is the sole business of poetry.
The rest's diversion: those holy or noble sentiments,
    the intricate ideas,
The love, lust, longing: reasons, but not the reason.

JESSIE BRENNAN Inside The Green Backyard (Opportunity Area) *Cyanotype Inside The Green Backyard (Opportunity Area)* is an artwork in the form of an archive of over 100 cyanotypes (camera-less photographs) and more than 100 voices (oral recordings), which documents a 'community growing project' in Peterborough threatened by a proposed development by its owner, the City Council. Cyanotypes of everyday objects on the site (such as this sink plug washer) generate lasting visual traces, their indexical image captured on light-sensitive papers exposed directly to the sun. In the context of urban development, the garden is not simply a place of rest and repose from which to escape the world: it is a site for poetry, art, critical thought and action, in which democratic struggles for the 'right to the city' are contested and fought for.

KIT BOYD Another World *Etching and aquatint*

Inspired by the Antony and the Johnsons song of the same title, this elegiac image of an imaginary landscape distils the essence of the British countryside I love into another world. Finding refuge in the subconscious, I create images that are a balm to the harsh reality of our modern lives, and which I hope lead the viewer down winding paths into a protective, womb-like environment.

[He comes to your door]   Ann Fisher-Wirth

                He comes to your door
raw-boned   bare-knuckled
looking for anything
        rake your driveway wash your windows
offers to chop wood cut grass   *ma'am* soft-voiced
                                anything

and he gets to telling
        how   like the badger
                I burrowed me a place

        how he sets his clothes and tools
the jar of nails   the saw
            his blue-handled hammer
along a bench he built in the hillsides

and tucks his sheets
            smooths *the Bear Paw quilt*
        my meemaw made   it's hard

[opposite] MAUDE SCHUYLER CLAY Mississippi Delta, 2013

59

to keep things off the dirt
    but he doesn't mind the baby spiders
        them little white things in a filmy cloud
near the door

        He tells you about the bluetick hound
the horse he had as a kid
    the job he wants to get   mopping floors
        stocking shelves at the Jitney

        He rakes   takes pay
    doesn't want food
drinks a glass of water
     ma'am I got what I need in the earth

This is a poem from the project *Mississippi*, on which I am collaborating with the acclaimed Mississippi photographer, Maude Schuyler Clay. Maude's photograph comes first, followed by the poem. The poem does not have a title, but is referred to by its first line. Here is a short prose statement that contextualises the project:

In her recent memoir, *The Faraway Nearby*, the environmental writer Rebecca Solnit writes: 'A place is a story, and stories are geography, and empathy is first of all an act of imagination, a storyteller's art, and then a way of travelling from here to there.' Mississippi, where I have lived for the past twenty-eight years, suffers from severe environmental degradation that cannot be separated from its history of poverty and racial oppression. Yet the state also possesses great natural beauty and a rich and complex culture, one interwoven from the many voices that have made up its identity. *Mississippi* explores both this degradation and this beauty.

I have come to understand the poems in this project as explorations of voice in its Mississippi plenitude and variety. Recently on Facebook, someone snarkily commented that though we hear people say things like *might could* and *aks*, 'That's not English.' I completely disagree. I honour the voices, no matter whose they are, both white and African-American. I love the rich orality of Mississippi culture, and have tried to express it. To write these poems, I listen to the voices that haunt the land. Out of silence, they emerge.

Afterworld

Susan Richardson

Here, all animals are equal,
equal in extinction.

The Moa, long ago
an Is-No-More, dozes

with the Golden Toad;
the Aurochs shoulders

the load of the Great Auk.
The Quagga logs

all recent arrivals –
the Western Black Rhino,

shorn of her horn,
Lonesome George crawling

from the island of himself,
the Spix's Macaw clawing

at reports
of captive survivors.

The Pyrenean Ibex
takes vertiginous bets

on who's next –
the Caspian Tiger's

sage striped guess says
the Pygmy Three-Toed Sloth's

outpacing
himself, racing past

the red edge
of mangroves,

while dead glaciers wait
for the kiss

of the Snow Leopard's tread.
And look, here's

the Common Skate,
swimming against

the tide of her name,
cartilaginous kite

snarled in infinite
promises.

Tangents not Definitional Strategies
– Journal Extracts

3rd October 2015 Schull, Co. Cork, Ireland

Just read the 'Crookhaven' chapter of Peter Somerville-Large's *The Coast of West Cork* (1972, 1985; Appletree Press 1991 edition, Belfast). As with earlier chapters, the book's tone shifts between acknowledgement of the wrongs of English/British colonialism and a strange kind of apologia (consider Somerville-Large's 'heritage'). But my reservations over its 1972 datedness aside, it is a useful and fascinating 'local' history project of passing through (cycling) and longer-term connection. There's always the colonial intrusion and non-belonging, but also the acquired and default setting of land-connection and individualised enculturation (within the slippage of AngloIrishness). Some very useful points come out through anecdote – either through his meeting 'old timers' (turn-of-the-twentieth-century experiences recounted) or through 'being there' – stopping over, collecting details, personal experience. A dot-point encounter, maybe, creating a pattern of encounter. Consider the metaphor that might arise from such patterning of information and the 'pattern' of religious investment of (older) place. I have been researching patterns and find an interesting point of departure in Somerville-Large's noting:

> It [a place nearby here] used to be one of the objectives of a
> pattern, along with a nearby well famous for its cures, but
> today no one makes the pilgrimage.

Maybe quote this as epigraph to my 'Pattern' poem?

Another useful quote in itself, regarding Crookhaven Harbour which I have written much about in the past regarding its lookout towers and connection with Marconi:

> Mr Jim O'Driscoll, who is over eighty, can remember when 'you wouldn't drag your feet for sailors'. On one occasion he had seen four wind-jammers, grain ships from Australia, sheltering in the harbour with their masts rising over the hills. Ships like these made a wonderful spectacle as their canvases billowed while they luffed up into a westerly wind and waited for the pilot boat to drag them in. From Crookhaven the masters would telephone to their head offices for instructions. To which part in the British Isles would they take their cargoes?

I am intrigued by the uncritical use of the word 'spectacle' in this quote, especially in the context of serving the 'British Isles'. There's a narrative poem about the grain from the farm connected with my family, Wheatlands, in Western Australia, and the journey of that wheat to Crookhaven. The married-into side of my family come out of English roots and the Irish side of my family with their migration from the famine-wracked world of grainlessness to make farms on the west coast of Australia, part of the paradoxical colonialism that still can't be reconciled.

Went out to Crookhaven and Mizen Head at around 4.30pm today where we walked behind the village down a dead-end road to the further point of the head (you can go without going onto PRIVATE PROPERTY). A good walk with ideas for these overlapping and contra-indicative poems of place that are forming. Tracy took photographs and Tim frolicked. The cows were inquisitive and involved – difficult to commune with the condemned and walk on. S. and her friend M. were walking the causeway road alongside the tidal flats and she told us the causeway across the neck of Barleycove estuary/beach/inlet was impassable due to storm damage a few weeks before we arrived back. School kids had to be taken by tractor to the school bus but then the tractor got stuck – the kids will be talking about it for years! So we took the road back past the old quarry to Goleen and took the roundabout way to Mizen to catch the golden disc of sunlight out on the ocean. The saturation of *place*. I need to be imbued – saturated (again and again) – in a place to write it (again). Passing through – temporariness – has its own dynamic, but it requires anchor-points, place of knowledge and a semblance of 'familiarity' built over continual exposures, to formulate into language for me. And then passing through Toormore heading back to Schull we see two mute swans feeding on weed at low tide.

4th October 2015 Schull

Spent the afternoon out on the Beara Peninsula. Went all the way down to the Beara side of the Dursey Island cable car. Wild down there today – busy seas and strong wind. Saw a ring fort near Cahamere – perfect circle surrounded by raddled sheep. Its white oculus itself overlooked by a Martello tower from another high point. And near the turn-off to Dursey Island a wedge tomb. A concentration of spiritual dialectics now dressed as points on the map, as *points de repère,* but also intrinsic markers of familiarity of belonging. More than artefacts. But the working fields are also the fields of industry, of animals 'serving' masters. The cows don't smile for photographers, though they watch. It's possibly appropriate to talk of the polysituating human moving from place to place and building a complex model of exclusion and participation, of exile and belonging, of loss and hope; but outside the analogies of migrating animals and birds, of their polyvalent connections to the places they breed in, winter in, pass through and cross over, what of those animals and birds constrained to a field, a paddock, a shed, a cage? Even with animals whose lives might naturally have been highly 'local', each step is a movement that alters the nature of place itself and how that creature relates to that place. But when the cows' udders fill to bursting and the sticks of the humans and the dogs at their 'feet' urge them towards the 'relief' of the milking machines, the same array of journeys (depending on which field is being grazed) is available to them, the polysituating self and herd-self prescribed, denuded of its possibilities, its ontologies.

Later, passing over Tim Healy Pass, we were confronted by a shillelagh-waving old man who had stopped a car of tourists. As we were returning down the narrow, winding, sheep-raddled roads the 'crazy man' stood in front of us, waving his weapon. He asked if we were enjoying *his* mountain, and was clearly about to exact a toll when we said, in reply to one of his many intrusive questions, We live here. Where? he demanded. The Mizen. And where do you come from? Australia. And what do you do? I am a poet. He then looked at Tracy and said, And you? A poet, she responds. And then I add, And our boy here goes to school on the Mizen. Hmmm, he says, baring broken yellow teeth and edging threateningly towards me, playing the part of the authentic crazy keeper of the pass that he clearly deploys for 'outsiders', adding, Hmmm, okay, I can see you are a happy family... you can pass. And we did. Okay. The event. The reaction at the time. But in retrospect (even a few minutes later among ourselves) we must be careful how we read this interaction. He doesn't get the chance to put his case outside indirect discourse; nor does he get to describe the state of our teeth! It was, maybe, 'play', but it was also serious. He behaved and played the part of a Sweeneylike figure or mountain shaman or preserver of a construct of Celtic legitimacy of presence or whatever other imagining of authenticity he was drawing on. It's worth noting the Tim Healy Pass was cleared with famine labour. But he was also enacting an important critique of visitation and removal, of the fleeting contact, of a form of temporariness. He was going to make it either a financially exacting contact – the toll paid – or transcendent. As Tracy said, as a female, if she'd been on her own she would have found it a very threatening encounter. The gender implications over-ride most other things in this – the vehicle he had pulled over earlier contained young women whom he had cajoled (or threatened?) out of the car and whom he was berating and also illuminating with his knowledge of the environs (we might assume: who's to say he is of the area … who's to say how he acquired his information, his 'authenticity'?). There was fear on the women's faces as the water rushed under the stone bridge of the 'troll'. A complex portrait of place as fetish and place in the bones. The shillelagh was a fetish but also a brutal weapon.

I continue musing over our encounter today as the Angelus rings out.

Note 1: To Irish visitors of the pass does the Sweeney-shaman-crazy man sell himself as someone über-local – the signature of that place specific? Does he sell himself as conduit, a medium, a transitional figure between the 'Irish' and 'The Others'? Is the presence across the curtain of life-death registered in his being, a changeling to be encountered and negotiated? Does he believe or is he hoping to encounter superstition to exploit?

Note 2: Does he store these encounters away in himself or converse (in say, the pub, shillelagh resting against the bar!) about his encounters? Does it legitimise his role among 'locals', his peers? Is he from elsewhere in Ireland and has 'adopted' Tim Healy pass as his own, or is he a lifer there? We've been over the pass many times over the years but have never seen him before.

Note 3: The tourist who has his/her photo taken with the accoster (who 'sells' his experience of isolation in Ireland to an American or Australian or Canadian of Irish heritage) to legitimise their own 'journey back' to the iceberg of their polysituatedness, the massive under-the-water imagined presence of belonging. In the romanticising of connection to place, this 'crazy man' figure becomes 'quaint' and part of their own authentication at the expense of the person who, aggressive as he was, was also clearly troubled and possibly quite mentally and physically unwell.

5th October 2015 Schull 12.30 pm

Went to go for my walk but the rain continues to come down hard. Will wait, though I am always walking in the rain over the Mizen. Almost finished reading the Somerville-Large book – he tries hard to be liberal-minded and often succeeds in elevating above his own origins and contradictory belongings as old Anglo-Irish. I consider this, as with all such books, an example of the fluid, mobile (literally in the case of this bike journey), polysituatedness. The poet who 'visits' places in the hope of making art does much the same – an expectation is there before leaving, then a process of encounter and reconsideration takes place. The points de repère/contacts are all pre-envisaged to some extent – hearing about other journeys, reading travel guides, family stories, a visit to such places earlier in life ...); all are in some ways 'known', expected, but also engaged with afresh and loaded with the expectation of adding to a knowledge base (discovery, surprise) at the points of passing through (and pause, hesitation, inspection, engagement, dialogue) and later in the telling, the recounting. The book is part-written before it is begun. Arterial, anatomical. Immersion of self into the organism of community and belonging, requiring acknowledgement of the colonial presence.

I feel no call of a 'Mother Country'. I have many heritages: Irish,

Scots, Cornish, English, Huguenot. I am what some term an 'Anglo-Celtic Australian'. But what I feel calling me is place-specific. I connect to land, which does not mean I have claim on that land. Maybe it's my temporariness that makes me long to be close to certain rocks and plants, animals and rivers, dry places and the wet. I am estranged from what most draws me. It is never my land. I am landless and I own nothing. I want to own nothing. I cannot own anything. I ask permission to stay wherever I am, even where I was born. Here, as a famine-migrant 'blowback', I ask permission where the dead of my family are buried in vast numbers. It's the rocks and the plants and the birds and the insects and the presence of something a long way back when animism was not merely synthesis but also respect. But animism knows no limitations of time: the presences are always there, but the damage done to the living world is more erasure than even deep belief can withstand. It is the respect for a place as thing-in-itself that interests me – more than the sum of its human parts.

I think back to some months ago when, after the long slow journey overland across Australia, I stood with Tracy and Tim looking at the small model of a lighthouse inland at Cape Clear, a hamlet in rural Victoria. And now I look across to Cape Clear Island from which many of the Irish 'settlers' who made that town in Victoria came, escaping almost certain death in the famine pits of here. And we wound down to Piggoreet where the gold workings offered hope in the weirding landscape, which they killed to make their 'freedoms'. All is invasion. All is undoing and disrespect. All is desperation and hope.

There are no easy formulaics.

Jam Tree Gully is always a resonating, echoing 'centre' for me – I am on the arms of its spirals. And in Hong Kong, walking from the heights down through the banyan trees to the skyscrapers and harbour and all contradictions in a place once full of cobras (still plentiful in surrounds) and the fake junk plying the harbour and Rome and the oculus of the Pantheon and the mining of copper on Cape Clear Island and neolithically up behind us in the Mount Gabriel range and here, here, here. I collate acknowledging the cost of passing, of temporariness, bringing the cost to the poem, the alteration of the hand that writes the poem.

Crossing the Irish Sea and Blake's Illustration to Dante's Hell Cantos 7 and 8

John Kinsella

At sea again. Past the harbour light,
headland's hold broken. Ink flows
like BP's sponsorship of The Arts.

Artefacts. The ship lolls through
phosphorescence. I hear gentle bell-
like tinkling in the closet and think

of Tracy's big bells in her Tübingen
poems, and I think of Slessor's elegy,
the haunting harbour bells. Source.

It sends me mad. I pull open the door
to find metal coat-hangers, *les extrêmes
se touchent*, touch, striking as windchimes

as the nightswell rocks. I separate
them, the hangers, three spread
evenly across the beam, but the swell

lifts and they find each other again.
Resounding. The cabin's mini-fridge
is stocked with two oranges and an

apple. An astrology. And so we return,
synecdoche of oars to the wavelets,
last white horses hunted down.

Rougher. Stars steady through portholes
to build by, currents feeding sepia wash.
Deep below, trucks and cars chained down.

And where the wind blows to collect
the gifts of Sellafield, feeder, and Easter
1916 celebrations still restless in Dublin.

Shimmering act of ongoing violence.
The Simpson's three-eyed fish is triumphant
in its misery, salmon finding the sea,

spumes of radiant spray rising over
the decks, the strands, the rocky pincers.
O glory of Technetium 99 in ranks

of seaweed, 3000 microsieverts exposé
for each and every soul, damned discharge
reprocessing phytoplankton O radio-

nuclides in sediment O plutonium
caesium Sellafield sell a field Seinfeld
(to catch your attention, rerun by rerun)

Phlegyas reckons it will be a calm crossing
with distant light dragging us on, the towers
of New York splendid in conceptualist

sails raised and full, twin moons
smothering with nurture, wealth bubbling
to the surface through the hot goo

just as sea scouts and yachts on the Canning
when I walked the white sands of childhood,
slush pouring out of the drains, the exquisite mire.

The Islands

Katrina Naomi

are mythical, maybe even a myth.
Uppermost is old Berkeley's metaphysics
of whether what you haven't seen
can be said to exist. Everyone speaks
of the islands in awed, hushed tones –
even my excitable friends – inspiring
a reverence; this, despite the islands'
apparent feudalism, great expense
and my friends' sea sickness. There's talk
of white sand, rare birds and no cars.
Do you see what I mean about the mythical?
And my new friend slips away towards
the islands, drawn, she says, by the promise
of hedgerows, rare seaweeds and the paucity
of people – even in August, if you know
where to go. I've only seen a film,
some blurry photos but *seen* nothing
myself. And then, coming over the hill
on the bus to St Just – a series of lumps
on the horizon – the islands appear,
and are gone. Every morning, I listen
for the three horns of the 9.15 sailing

to another world, to those islands,
that may, or may not, exist.

Spawn

Kim Goldberg

Under the bluest sky of the year, I stood at the edge of my world
and watched the flickerflashing churn of brimming life, the sea gone
white with sperm – the stench and smoky spew
of diesel-powered winches winding in their nets, beating
out the fish. I watched the shooting stars cascade into
the darkened hold to be later stripped of roe for
Japanese markets. The yawning emptiness between electrons
in the salty air – packed tight today with sirens' wail
and squaggling song from four thousand gulls and brant
aloft beyond the endless snowy drift of milt
whipped thick and scattered into bands of froth along a tideline
with no vanishing point at all.
All of this on the same day that the radioactive cloud
from Japan's nuclear disaster was scheduled to reach our shore –
all of us together in this self-made retroactive cloud
with no vanishing point at all.
We tipped and scattered clamshells in the froth, our lifeline
lost beyond the endless rift cleaving molten
rock and magma from four thousand songs and plants.
The salty air packed tight today with sirens' wail
in Japanese markets, while the yawning emptiness of our elections
echoes in a darkened hold to be later stripped and sold

as fish bait. We watched the shooting stars cascade into
a diesel-flowered meadow binding all our heads, beating
while it burned until the stench and smoky spew
was traded for the flickerflash of atomic churn. And the sea was gone
under the bluest sky of the year, as we stood at the edge of our world.

'Spawn' was written on March 18, 2011, on the day that was the
confluence of two significant ecological events: the peak of the annual
herring spawn on the east coast of Vancouver Island, and the arrival on
the Pacific Coast of North America of the radioactive cloud from the
Fukushima disaster. I chose to document it with a loose palindrome
to reflect the collision of two realities. – KG

Midnight Oil

Sheryl St. Germain

how to speak of it
this thing that doesn't rhyme
or pulse in iambs or move in predictable ways
like lines
or sentences

how to find the syntax
of this thing
that rides the tides
and moves with the tides and under the tides
and through the tides
and has an underbelly so deep and wide
even our most powerful lights
cannot illuminate its full body

this is our soul shadow,
that darkness we cannot own
the form we cannot name

and I can only write about it at night
when my own shadow wakes me, when I can feel
night covering every pore and hair follicle, entering eyes
and ears, entering me like Zeus, a night I don't want
on me or in me, and I dream of giving birth
to a rusty blob of a child who slithers out of me,
out and out and won't stop slithering, growing and darkening,
spreading and pulsing between my legs
darkening into the world

*

what it might feel like to be a turtle, say,
swimming in the only waters you have ever known
swimming because it is the only way you move through the world
to come upon this black bile
a kind of cloying lover

a thing that looks to you
like a jellyfish, so you dive into it and try to eat it
but it covers your fins so they can't move as before
and there is a heaviness on your carapace and head
that wasn't there before, and you are blind
in the waters of your birth

When the summers got too hot even for those of us born in New Orleans, so hot that our ancestors' bones sweated and complained in their vaults, my father would decide it was time, and the family would pile into the station wagon and drive down to Grand Isle, where we'd run along the beach into the Gulf as if into a lover's arms, smash into the salty waves, swim until the sun went down and we were red as boiled crawfish.

Mother would have made a pungent crab salad, with quarters of crab marinated in garlic and olive oil, lemon and celery. Sometimes we'd have boiled shrimp or crabs. The grownups would stay up drinking and playing cards at night while we slept the sweet sleep of children who don't yet know what stygian rivers run in their veins. Exhausted from swimming, hair still damp and smelling like the Gulf, we'd huddle together in the big bed on the screened porch. The smell and sound of the waves rocked us to sleep, dreams of pelicans and gulls and flying fish filled our heads and hearts, and we were content.

On rainy days when we couldn't swim my father taught me how to play pool in one of the hulking bars that used to front the beach. The bar's gone now, like the house we stayed in, destroyed by hurricanes that wipe out

every human-made thing   every few years.

*

Oiled Birds, edited from Wikipedia:

*Penetrates plumage, reduces insulating ability, makes birds
vulnerable to temperature fluctuations, less buoyant in water.
Impairs bird's abilities to forage and escape predators. When
preening, bird ingests oil that covers feathers, causing kidney
damage, altered liver function, digestive tract irritation. Foraging
ability is limited. Dehydration, metabolic imbalances. Bird will
probably die unless there is human intervention.*

*

I'm looking at an old photo of my brother, right after he got out
of prison.   He's twenty, sitting on a beach chair at Grand Isle,
looking gaunt and pale, but smiling.
It was the first place my mother thought to take him
when she feared the grime and shame of that other place
might have tarnished his heart too deeply.

She knew he loved this island, where simple things
like saltwater and clean beaches,
birds and fish, crabs,
might act like containment booms,
keep the demons away.

He'd die a few years later,
his liver polluted with what he thought
would make the world bearable,
and a few years after him
my father would go
from that same staining.

Now, when I look at these beaches I love,
greasy with oil as far as I can see,
when I think of how this island
and its marshes should act like filters,
I think of my father and brother,
I think this is what
their livers must have looked like
as they moved toward the end, darkening,
becoming pebbly with disease, finally
too black with blight
to filter
anything.

*

It's June in Pittsburgh where I live now, hot and muggy,
and it feels like a day my father would've said *let's go.*

*

People don't want to look at the pictures anymore of the birds
and turtles, the fish, the oiled beaches
                    they want to go on to something else
they don't want to hear about the old fishermen
            who may never fish again
                    the ones being trained to clean up instead of fish

        It's an old story, really, how we always dirty what we love,
                and I'm tired too, have seen way too many pictures
                of oiled birds and the oiled waters of this dear place

            and I've heard way too many pundits and politicians
                    and newsmen analyse, blame and predict

            and jokemen joke:
                    let's call the Gulf *the Black Sea.*

Dear CNN: even the devil would bore us
if he was on 24 hours a day

there are times we need silence
as much as we need news

or a poem that creates a silence
in us where we can feel again

*

How people from Louisiana have described the oil:

Brown and vivid orange globs. Tar balls. Thick gobs. Red waves.
Deep stagnant ooze. Clumps of tar. Consistency of latex paint.
Sheets of foul-smelling oil. Patches of oil. Caramel-coloured oil.
Tide of oil. Red brown oil. Rainbows of Death. Waves of gooey tar
blobs. Bruised internal organs of a human body. Heavy heavy
slickoil. Oil sheen. Oily stench. Melted chocolate.

*

An eye for an eye, my father might say,
a tooth for a tooth.

Let's ask those responsible,
and some of those are us

to walk deep out into the waters
of this once beautiful island,
the waters that once teemed with speckled trout,
oysters, shrimp,
let's ask them to walk far out into it,
to swim out with long sweeping strokes,

and then,
when they are thick and covered
with the stuff,   when it's in their hair and blinding
them, stopping up their ears and mouths,
when it's sticking to every pore
in their body,

then
let them try to swim back

then
let them try to explain

What Kingdom Without Common Feasting?

Jake Campbell

It is a miserable Thursday morning in early March. I have just crossed the river Wear and am driving through Shiney Row towards Bournmoor to interview Graham Martin, son of the late poet, William Martin. This is where the relatively flat part of south-west Sunderland begins to give way to the hills of County Durham. Across Herrington Country Park the landscape rises, topped with former miners' cottages, tracing the way people lived and worked here not long ago. I turn my eyes back to the road, reminding myself that smashing into the back of another motorist while wrapped up in considering the latent psychogeographic vestiges of the Durham coalfield en route to researching a poet would be too ludicrous a thing to have to explain on any insurance claims.

Just visible amid blanket clouds is the imposing folly of Penshaw Monument, built in 1844 in memory of John George Lambton, the first Earl of Durham. The Lambton family, and the hills of East Durham and Wearside where they lived, will always be associated with the legend of the Lambton Worm, a giant dragon-like creature which, it is said, terrorised the people and livestock of the area and was heroically slain by (another) John Lambton, with the assistance of a local witch's divination.

The legend of the Lambton Worm is well known in these parts. In schools across England's North East, children still learn about the fearful worm; in Sunderland city centre there is a Wetherspoon's pub named after it; and most people can recite at least the chorus from the folk song inspired by the story: 'Wisht, lads, had ya gobs, I'll tell yous aall an aafull story/Wisht, lads, had ya gobs, I'll tell yous aboot the worm.'

Like many other local curiosities, the Lambton Worm is referred to in the work of William Martin. Arriving at his son's house just as the clouds begin to lift, I sit down with Graham, who hands me a cup of coffee and begins telling me about his father's life and work. It is a conversation of no more than an hour and a quarter, but during it I become convinced that Martin was an important poet whose work grew from the very hills and mines that surrounded him. Nourished by the myths and legends of these landscapes, and complemented by a wider appreciation of international politics and religious iconography, they sustained his idea of a poetics which drew people together in universal feast. As a line from 'Durham Beatitude' would have it, 'What Kingdom without common Feasting?'

William Martin's 1983 book *Cracknrigg* contains two poems which are not really poems at all: though bearing their author's original titles, they are in fact quotes from sources which illuminate the collection's themes and speak more broadly of the man writing them, the community he was part of, and how he saw his own role as a poet within it. They bear quoting in full, as epigraphs of sorts to this essay. The first, 'Out of the Whirlwind':

I believe that the food sharing hypothesis

is a very strong candidate for explaining

what set early hominids on the road to modern

man ... Hunting-and-gathering was a permanent

and stable feature of our biological evolution

through Homo erectus to early Homo sapiens

and finally to modern man. Given the importance

of hunting-and-gathering through the many

thousands of generations of our forebears, it

may well be that this way of life is an
indelible part of what makes us human.

Richard E. Leakey *The Making of Mankind*[1]

Secondly, halfway through the book, 'Left Side', part of 'Triptych':

As the strike had continued for some time,
and the men and their families were in
consequence suffering from the effects of
hunger, it was suggested that every man
attending the meeting from pits which were
still at work, and who could afford it, should
bring a loaf of bread to the meeting. This
caused a great attraction, and the meeting
was very numerously attended. Hundreds of
loaves were laid out in the field, and were
formed into letters making the texts:–
"Go thou and do likewise" "a friend in need
is a friend indeed" "help one another"

Richard Fynes *The Miners of Northumberland
and Durham* pub. 1873[2]

William – Bill, as his friends knew him – Martin was born in
Silksworth, County Durham (now part of Sunderland, Tyne and
Wear) in 1925. He died in 2010, the year that a coalition govern-

ment, spearheaded by the Conservatives, entered the halls of Westminster and set about unravelling the social fibres of the world that he had lived amongst and wrote about.

What is immediately noticeable when first looking through Bill's books – four full collections and two pamphlets – is the intricacy of his practice and how references, allusions and even the very structures of some his poems are indebted to myriad other sources. It is said that a book should not be judged by its cover, but in the case of Bill's work, the covers – and indeed his illustrations within many of them – are a fundamental part of his oeuvre: a poetics which takes wide inspiration, from the street-songs and games of his youth to the working class solidarity of his adulthood, melding it together to form what is not far-fetched to describe as a *vision*; an holistic awareness of the world imbued in the past, but always aware of its becoming something else.

I was born 63 years after Bill Martin, 11 miles away, in South Shields. I entered the world just over three years after the end of the 1984–85 miners' strike. Too young to remember in real-terms its fallout on the jobs, industrial landscapes and people it was fought over, I do remember (though not in such abstract terms) the benefits of unrestricted economic growth, technological advancement and general laissez-faire capitalism that lasted until the wheels began to fall off in 2008, during my time as an undergraduate.

My first impression that recession was something that could directly impact me was while working for Royal Worcester and Spode, the makers of fine china, within a concession of the Debenhams department store in Chester. I spent the brief months I worked there, before the firm entered administration and eventually closed, day-dreaming of the poets I was reading on my course. Bloodaxe Books' seminal anthology, *Staying Alive*, was a set text during my undergraduate years, and through it, I was introduced to vital, energetic, witty, bold, humorous and very *real* poems.

Bill Martin came later, as I was preparing my application for my PhD. At the time, I was reading the 'big' names in North East poetry: Basil Bunting, Katrina Porteous, Barry MacSweeney and others. It was not until an early supervisory meeting, when handed a copy of *Cracknrigg*, that Bill Martin's work appeared on my radar. Published by Taxvs, a now-defunct press from County Durham, the book looked, and crucially *felt*, different. Bibliophiles will know precisely what I mean when I refer to the earthen quality of the paper, or laud over the just-right style of the font and typesetting, or marvel at the decorative intricacy of the cover imagery.

One's general sense of reading Bill's books, stripped largely as they are of the subjective 'I' voice, is the creation of a rich, parallel world portrayed via an oral, storytelling tradition which speaks of and about the community, looking to figures from spirituality and myth for guidance, but ultimately intending for a plethora of ordinary voices to be heard for the advancement of the common good.

As somebody who grew up with the implicit mantra – attributed to Margaret Thatcher – that 'there is no such thing as society', and whose first years of serious study of poetry centred largely around the first-person-narrated poem, coming to Bill's work was, admittedly, a struggle. I should caveat those two statements by saying that I had a fantastic childhood, and so far have had an excellent early adulthood, in large part thanks to the political and economic doctrines of the past thirty years; and that poets who write in the first-person (myself included) are not necessarily writing work which is substandard. In fact, largely, the opposite is true: a first-person insight can be just as revelatory as a third-person one, and a single point-of-view can say as much as a collective one. However, to read books like *Cracknrigg* is to feel something of what has been lost in the North East – and in British and Western society more generally – over the past three or four decades: that poetry exists both for the head and the heart, for the ear and the eye, and for the individual with all of their quirks and concerns, and for the society they are part of and how it views itself within the world.

*

Bill Martin lived most of his life in sight of Tunstall Hills in Sunderland, a place he affectionately referred to as the 'Maiden Paps', for their appearance as a woman's breasts springing from the ground. For Bill, this represented the Goddess in the landscape. The 'Maiden Paps' are a recurrent motif throughout his poetry. In his last collection, *Lammas Alanna* (Bloodaxe, 1999), a 12-section poem, 'Abuba Bide', contains the following lines:

> Her hill-breast flesh
> Glows above corn ripening
>
> She oversees the harvest coming soon
>
> We play around climbing the Rocky
> Or rolling down tender grass slopes
> To a strip of strong blue sea
> Smudged with chimney smoke
>
> Colliers sailing off
> Leaving her emptying mines behind[3]

Needless to say, there is a lot going on here. A geographical familiarity with the coastline of Sunderland, or knowledge of the Durham coalfield, is not necessary to understand Martin's lines, 'a strip of strong blue sea/Smudged with chimney smoke//Colliers sailing off'. Nor do we need to reach too far to understand the metaphor of 'her emptying mines behind' to appreciate that Martin is comparing a harvest, traditionally associated with the 'corn ripening', to the stripping of carbon power in the form of coal from the 'hill-breast flesh' of his beloved Maiden Paps.

Despite what we now understand to be the ruinous effects of carboniferous capitalism on our environment, the image conveyed here is idyllic: a willing Goddess 'oversees the harvest coming soon' and appears benevolent to the children who 'play around' her 'tender grass slopes'. Femininity, motherhood, even early sexual awakenings are all connoted here, but the effect in totality is not cynical; not an abasement of the feminine at the hands of corrupting male influence, but a harmonious scene in which children are part of nature, nature is part of industry, and industry is part of landscape.

In an earlier section, Martin reaches further, linking the self with the community; the sacred as a guiding light through the temptations of potentially profane forces. Again, it is necessary to quote in full:

> A song comes into the ear
> From somewhere about
>
> It is marra music that gets louder
> Brass voices tenor and bass fill the morning
>
> And its beat bloods the heart
> Of many following
>
> She is singing in long streets
> Calling all like the piper

But not to be lost

It is a way of arms linking
A dance of life[4]

Here, perhaps, it does become useful to have knowledge of the Durham coalfield and an understanding of some of the North East dialect words that Martin weaves into his work. In Martin's own words at the notes at the back of his pamphlet, *Tidings of our Bairn-sea*: 'By "Marra" I mean the man not the vegetable. Equal, like, kind. Workmate, friend, comrade.'[5] 'Marra music', then, is the music played by the brass bands that, to this day, form the musical accompaniment to the marching (ex)colliery workers and their families as they wind their way from the pit villages to converge on Durham Cathedral, at the annual Miners' Gala.

I have heard it said that in some mining communities the term 'marra' referred to the physical proximity with which men worked alongside each other underground: so close they might as well have been part of each other's bone marrow. Hence, 'marra'. I also like Martin's assertion, 'not the vegetable', because actually, when you consider the growth of marrows as vegetables, especially bearing in mind that they would have regularly been grown on allotments around the North East to supplement food in times of hardship during and post World War Two, they would have been planted close together, all nourished by the same land and all going on to the dinner tables of people who had an intimate connection to where much of their food came from and an intimate understanding of what it was there to fuel: hard but skilled work, which saw workers' rights fought for, which saw community spirit championed, and which advocated 'unity is strength' over the atomised society of consumers that we have become.

Why, years after the pits closed in Great Britain, should the Durham Miners' Gala continue to thrive as one of Europe's greatest celebrations of social spirit, collective action and sustained trade union activism? Another pertinent question, one which I have asked myself regularly while writing my own poems, is 'Why should I, a man in his late twenties, a beneficiary of neoliberal economic policy, gravitate towards such an event?'

Robert Frost said that 'A poem begins with a lump in the throat'. The lump in the throat of many people right now, irrespective of whether or not they read and write poetry, is that this life is not enough. We are not satisfied by thousands of TV channels, by endless social media feeds, by rolling news of terrorist attacks and floods and cuts to local services. Why would we be? How, then, as poets, do we begin to broach these big topics? How do our poems contain enough of the driving force we call sentiment and marry it, in unique and original ways, with metaphors, couplets and syllables, to question our own place in it all?

*

It is a month since I met with Graham. Since then, he has sent me two books and seven CDs. There are hours of remastered old tape recordings of Bill discussing his life: his time in India during the War; his memories of the 'Big Meeting' (the Durham Miners' Gala); and conversations that I haven't yet had time to listen to, but include intriguing descriptions such as 'Tape 5: Anglo-Saxons and Black Madonnas; Tape 7: The Goddess'. There are many songs and poems, too: including 'Durham Beatitude', which features on the CD accompanying this book.

All of these esoteric allusions and niche historical sources chime with something Graham told me when he was remembering, with sadness, having to discard thousands of books from his father's study after his death. 'My Dad was a polymath: there were books on everything from Celtic Christianity and Gnosticism to the Dead Sea Scrolls.' When I ask Graham what happened to the books, he sighs and tells me most of them were put in a skip. 'The Lit and Phil (independent library in Newcastle) could only take so many, as could Oxfam.' I tell him that, as a reader and a writer, this feels like a massive shame, which he agrees with, but what could he do?

During my initial forays into researching Bill's poetry, I came across his annual summer solstice pilgrimage, from his home near Silksworth to Durham Cathedral. Keen to recreate the walk and find out more, I ask Graham about it.

'The walks were pilgrimages, yes, but also celebrations of landscape, people, place, traditions and industry. They were in honour of the "Haliwerfolc", the people of the Saint (Cuthbert) whose body was carried from Holy Island (Lindisfarne) around the north of England and eventually laid to rest at Durham Cathedral. Later, they became a sort of memoriam, for the suicide of my dad's friend, to remember his life and look back.'

The route follows old coal wagon ways, fields and B roads, to arrive at Durham on the longest day of the year, paying tribute to the dead and the living along the way. Notions of the 'Return' permeate the walk, which for Bill was emblematic of the cyclical nature of life and spoke to the social, environmental and spiritual concerns of his life and poetry; and whose boundaries I am increasingly finding, in both Bill's life and work and my own, interchangeable.

Walking in the footsteps of others is something that has interested me for a while now. Last summer, following Bede's Way through north Sunderland and South Tyneside, I co-led a group of around fifteen people on a trail between the twinned monasteries of St. Peter's and St. Paul's, seventh-century churches set up in Sunderland and Jarrow respectively by Benedict Biscop and later entrusted to the care of the Venerable Bede, the man who would write the first history of the English people.

Due to financial pressures – more or less symptomatic of the wider brunt of what has been referred to as the 'cultural desertification' of the North – the Bede's World museum in Jarrow, dedicated to the life and times of one of Europe's greatest scholars, has, at the time of writing in April 2016, been closed for two months, and may only reopen in the summer under a more commercially viable footing. I think it is nothing short of a scandal that some of the North's most important cultural assets are being left to rust or be covered in weeds because our self-serving government based in the South East wants to retain 'nice', 'quaint' or 'easy' bits of heritage and arts as little more than decoration for their huge, global finance magnet.

Bill's pilgrimage was a journey through a palimpsest: by following the men who had once processed Cuthbert's tomb through this landscape, he was able to conflate past and present, tying the various splintered histories of the area together in a vision of collective sanctum which he referred to as 'marradharma'. Talking about his memories of taking part in the summer solstice walks with his Dad, Graham remembers how Bill would pick up stones en route, and later deposit them, talisman-like, at the foot of Cuthbert's tomb. It is difficult to imagine somebody like George Osborne doing the same.

Considering both the physical and metaphysical implications of the walk – its route through a beautiful, historic landscape, its spiritual connections, and its convivial bringing together of people across times and spaces – I think back to my existential questioning, of what it is that should motivate and drive a poet in these fucked-up times, and I reach the only logical conclusion that I can, having spent months reading Martin's work: that the poet is not, and should not be, a lone operator.

'Poems should echo and re-echo against each other,' says Jack Spicer. 'They should create resonances. They cannot live alone any more than we can.'[6] The life and work of Bill Martin encapsulates this sentiment, though it is decidedly at odds with the current state of play. In Sunderland, as in many other parts of the 'United' Kingdom, more than 60% of people recently opted to leave the European Union. The referendum has exposed long-festering divisions in this country and, in places like the North East, a demonstrative electorate has sounded its fury at out-of-touch politicians of all stripes. As each year brings with it an increasing tirade of grim news and a corresponding wave of far-right vitriol, the North seems to shrink further from the concerns of those in the real Powerhouse, in the City and Home Counties. Deeply unsatisfied by the vast inequality of the status quo for at least thirty years, this North that I am from, live in and love is starting to turn on itself, looking for scapegoats and blaming those who are helpless and innocent. Common feasting feels a long way away.

*

It strikes me that the legend of the Lambton Worm is, at its core, a cautionary tale of the power of nature and its potential malevolent forces.

The young John Lambton, absent from mass to fish in the Wear, catches an unusually strong fish, which turns out to be a worm. Thinking little more of it, he places it in his sack, leaves the river, and eventually discards it down a well. John then goes away for seven years to fight in the crusades, while in the meantime, the worm grows in the well, emerging as a giant dragon-like beast, terrorising the locals, eating their young, butchering their sheep and cows, and only sated by gifts of milk presented in a trough at the gates of Lambton Hall.

Upon his return from the wars, now a noble and courageous knight, John is told that only he can kill the Worm. He visits a wise woman who tells him to ask the local blacksmith to fashion him a suit of armour adorned with spikes. Before he leaves to commence his duty, he is warned that, unless he also slays the first living thing he sees after seeing off the Worm, his family will be cursed for three generations and will not die in their beds. Swearing the oath, John sets out the next day, taking refuge on a stone in the middle of the Wear, where the Worm, unable to attack him from that angle, repeatedly slashes itself on his armour until it is chopped into pieces and sent floating, lifeless, downstream.

Sounding a victory call on his bugle so that his hounds might be released, John makes his way back to Lambton Hall. In the excitement, however, his servants allow John's father to pass, and it is he who he sees first. In the commotion, John sounds his bugle again, and eventually slashes one of his dogs. John's vow is broken, though, and three generations of Lambton men, as the wise woman foretold, did not die peacefully in bed.

There is reason to believe that the story of the Lambton Worm was invented by the Church as a warning to young children (or anyone else, for that matter) who might be tempted to skive off Sunday service. There are also overt Arthurian similarities: in the folk song that has become the most commonly-known version of the story, John is hailed as a hero who kept the bairns from harm. The curse placed on the Lambton family by the wise woman (who would have almost certainly been declared at best a heretic, or more likely hunted down as a witch) is not mentioned in the song; indeed she is not mentioned at all. Instead, John is presented as a selfless man who chooses to come back from Palestine to defend his people of his own accord.

Whatever the case, and however the story came into being and however it has been manipulated since, the fact that it has continued for so long is surely worth dwelling on. What evils threaten us now, and how do we approach their banishment? It seems that little has changed: we whip ourselves up into frenzy, we carpet bomb, we shoot first and ask searing philosophical questions rarely. This is how Bill Martin alludes to the Lambton Worm, in section 30 of his long poem, 'Wiramutha [Wearmouth] Helix':

Ancient bairns cry ancient lament...
Templar knight caaled back from Palestine...

Sybil's killing advice and warning...
Death on spiked armour

Older than John-Michael
Our shiny flawed hero

Ancient bairns
Cry ancient lament.[7]

This is quite different to the folk song I grew up with. Sybil, who we can presume to be the wise woman or witch, is here named, assuming the role of a sage, or prophet. John is 'shiny', as we expect, but also 'flawed', and the 'ancient bairns', who we must take to be the children the Worm ate, appear to be, if not sympathetic towards the Worm, then at least sympathetic towards the violent circumstances in which it was brutally murdered and the tragic loss of their brothers, sisters and friends – their marras.

Appearing in *Hinny Beata* (sub-title: *An Exploration of the Ancient Feminine*), 'Wiramutha Helix' draws on a circumnavigation of significant places in or near Sunderland. In Martin's own words:

For many years I walked from my home near Tunstall Hills (Maiden Paps) past Thorn Hill, where there is a Convent of Mercy, to

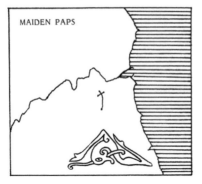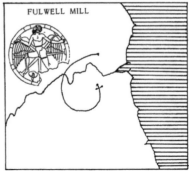

Left to right: Maiden Paps; Fulwell Mill; Penshaw Monument; North Sea, all from 'Wiramutha Helix' by William Martin

my work at a local hospital. Looking at a map one day I realised that there were a number of major features around the town that were four miles from a centre at Thorn Hill, e.g. Warden Law, which is connected with the Dun Cow legend and is reputed to be the last resting place of Saint Cuthbert before Durham. From this grew the idea of the Helix, to include further historic and geographic sites.[8]

Using what academics might refer to as a perambulatory methodology, or what the zeitgeist might term 'psychogeography', Bill Martin was a man who, walking through his home town, travelled into the past to trace its common histories and significant events, as well as its idiosyncrasies, and map them onto his contemporaneous experience of a changed – and ever-changing – North East.

Unless we look for them, our common histories will exist at best as vestiges, and at worst, remain unknown, unrecognisable or warped for malicious ends. Where does this leave poets? How might our poems 'echo and re-echo against each other' today? How might we navigate our way through this Yeatsean 'terrible beauty' which seems to be being born?

Many of the poems we start out writing begin in the swell of what

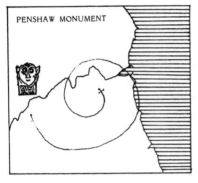
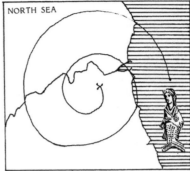

the poet Sean O'Brien has referred to as 'a tidal wave of anecdote'. These well-meaning, often skilfully-crafted poems are nonetheless so similar to other poems in their formulaic style of 'I-saw-this-then-it-made-me-think-this-which-was-like-that-and-then-I-had-this-revelation-and-it's-like-this-amazing-thing-wow!' that they can pale into insignificance. Many of them, of course, are fantastic; some will even be read in anthologies for decades to come.

I don't think social media, with its recourse to easily facilitating broadcasts of every element of a person's life, from the simple to the sublime, has helped stem the flow of O'Brien's wave of anecdote. It follows that a person – especially a young person, a digital native shall we say – who has lived most of their life with access to a hand-held device which can capture thousands of images and, with a few swipes of a screen, project them into the social universe for validation, may view their own poems as functioning in the same mode: as micro-fictional snippets in which, yes, something happened or was witnessed, and briefly it was, like, epic, but it was one small thing, captured lazily before being moved on to the next, and in retrospect, even a few months later, wasn't even that great.

Social media rewards freshness, further clicks and constant

manipulation. Social media wants ephemeral, fleeting moments of anecdote, because they can be tagged and shared, and ultimately algorithmised and sold back to the source from which they came in the form of targeted advertising. A small amount of this is fine. But in incessant, bite-size chunks, which are rarely chewed let alone digested, it is difficult, if not impossible, to genuinely contemplate.

Poetry is different. The 'always-on' culture – our emails, WhatsApps, tweets and countless other inane notifications buzzing our smartphones, compelling us to keep abreast of a virtual world at the expense of the real one – is different to the slow reading culture that poetry fosters. It is true that poetry has been taught badly in schools, but I refute the easily-reached-for claim, and I've lost count of the number of times I've heard it, that declares the reason people don't read poetry is 'it's hard'. Of course it's hard! It's meant to be. If social media is a thousand tiny pieces of broken glass, each refracting in different ways, poetry is the uniting force which brings them all together, levitates them in front of your face, and makes you look at your own reflection and the world behind it.

I like to read and write poetry because doing so requires that I focus, really devote my attention to the alchemical beauty of – nodding to Coleridge – putting the best words in the best order. Writing a good poem is a mutually-enriching process of spending many hundreds of hours of careful reading, thought, drafting and re-drafting. I enjoy scribbling in my notebook some initial thoughts or lines, usually in prose, then leaving those thoughts to rest in my brain, to germinate in the dark, so that when I come back days, weeks, sometimes even months or years later, my thoughts have coalesced with my ongoing reading, and the poem, gradually, begins to take shape. When I type a tweet or an email, I do so with little consideration that the message I am writing is perfected: I tap my keyboard and fire it off into the ether. Occasionally I retrospectively discover typos, or realise that my syntax is off, or a sentence here or there just doesn't quite sit. The point is, I do it rapidly and I do it regularly. When I write a poem – which really means when I spend months re-writing a poem – I pore over every detail: I consider synonyms; I scan the rhyme scheme, judging whether certain words should be moved or deleted, to help the poem flow; I play with different titles. In short, when I write poetry, I do it much more consciously, so that the finished poem (if it can ever truly be finished) says precisely what *needed* to be said, not what I fleetingly thought was important online, and which more often than not was, in hindsight, trivial, banal or outright unnecessary.

Where the internet and social media can feel like a never-ending display of fireworks – glitzy and impressive, but ultimately transitory lights punctuating darkness – the reading and writing of poetry is the long game: the growth of a tree, becoming thicker each year, always dependant on the rings that came before, hefted into something larger, much more solid and drawing nourishment from the soil and the atmosphere while simultaneously giving life back. I may make a topical statement online (and in the wake of the EU referendum, I and many others have done so, repeatedly) but when I write a sequence of poems about the zeitgeist, I do so in a much more considered way: that pays respect to nuance, that factors in contradiction, and that attempts, above all else, to be really honest.

Apart from the obvious anachronism, I don't think Bill Martin would have had a Facebook account. No, I think he would have encouraged his friends to do more of what he did at the summer solstice, or on his circular walks around Sunderland. He would have brought his 'marras' together, outside and away from the isolating, silent vacuums and political echo-chambers of their smartphones and tablets, encouraging them to feast as one, to learn from each other and pay respect to difference. He would have got them to walk from one place to another; to be present in a landscape, contemplating its layers of history; to listen to the birds sing; to look for butterflies and wild flowers; to scan vistas from the tops of hills and imagine what stories might be contained beneath them; to carry pebbles and think about their journey through geology towards becoming bedrock or cairns; to join together and walk, write, sing. If asked what poetry meant to him, what it is for and should aim to do, I think he would have quoted you from one of his own lines: 'It is a way of arms linking/A dance of life.'

Wiramutha Helix, from epigraph 'Wiramutha Helix'
by William Martin

Notes

1. William Martin, 'Out of the Whirlwind', in *Cracknrigg* (Taxvs: Durham, 1983), p.7.
2. William Martin, 'Left Side', in *Cracknrigg* (Taxvs: Durham, 1983), p.43.
3. William Martin, 'Abuba Bide', in *Lammas Alanna* (Bloodaxe: Newcastle upon Tyne, 1999), p.107.
4. Ibid, p.106.
5. William Martin, *Tidings Of Our Bairnsea* (Published for the Wearmouth 1300 Festival: Durham, 1973), p.43.
6. Jack Spicer, Second Letter from *Admonitions*, quote accessed online: http://bit.do/letter2, 6th April 2016.
7. William Martin, 'Wiramutha Helix' in *Hinny Beata* (Taxvs: Durham, 1987), page number not given, but section 30.
8. Ibid, 'Notes' (page number not given).

Salt worker, Sečovlje

Jane Lovell

There is a point at which he leans
and pauses, and the sun bleaches
the edges from the salt pile,
the wooden rake, the tracks and carts
with their drapery of halite.

His face gleams like flowstone,
eyes fix upon a line
pinning tool huts all the way
to the horizon,
                a land
brimming sea and salt-blooms
above carpets of petola,
quiet pans of algae, gypsum, clay
where egrets pick their way
through cubes of sky.

He is listening to the voice
of the salt, the tinkering of the sea
as it abandons its minerals
at his feet.

Terns blow in from the ocean.
Swallows sweep the Giassi channel
past the new museum.
The sea drifts out to join the sky.

He does not move.
A rime of salt blisters his lips,
gathers in his desiccated bones.

Eight centuries of shift and hiss;
he closes his eyes,
balances against the light.

*The Sečovlje salts flats are the northernmost salt flats in the Mediterranean.
The salt is produced in the traditional way based on a 700-year-old method
that seeks to harmonise human activity with the natural environment.
Over the centuries, a unique habitat has formed for halophytic plants and
animals and migrating birds.*

Slaughterer   Vahni Capildeo

The tears curled from the cattle's eyes, their horns curled back, their
coats curled like frost-ferns on windshields or the hair on the heads
of Sikandar's soldiers. Two of my grandfather's sons, when he knew
he was dying, took him from his bed. They supported him out the
doorway so he could say goodbye to his favourite cattle. The cattle
wept. They knew him. They are not like cattle here. They live among
the household and on the hills, which are very green, and they eat
good food, the same food as the household, cut-up pieces of
leftover chapatti.

You do not get stories like that in books. I am telling you
because you only have things to read. Whenever anybody tried to
make me read a book or anything, I would fall asleep; my head
would just drop.

What is the use of reading books? What can you do after that
but get an office job? Do my friends who stayed at school earn as
much as me? They all have office jobs; could they do a job like
mine? Could they slaughter for seventy hours without getting tired
or needing to sleep?

It was hard at first. I used to dream the cattle. They would
come to me with big eyes, like mothers and sisters. After a few
weeks, they stopped coming to me in dreams. After about five years,
I stopped feeling tired: I do not need to sleep. We do three or four

thousand a day in Birmingham, only a thousand a night in Lancaster.

Tonight I am going to Lancaster. I will talk to you until Lancaster. Where are you from? You are lying on me. No, where are your parents from? Are you lying on me? I came here as a teenager, and at once they tried making me read. How old are you? Why do you only have things to read? I am sorry I am talking to you. You have brought things you want to read. Beautiful reader, what is your name?

You can feel the quality of the meat in the animal when it is alive: the way its skin fits on its flesh. You can feel the quality of life in the meat. The cattle here are not good. They inject them. Their flesh is ahhh.

Look, look how beautiful. I will show you pictures of the place. Look, it is very green.

Notes on the Use of the
Austrian Scythe

Emma Must

You can no more lend a man your scythe
than you can lend him your false teeth,
so take my day instead, borrow this meadow.
I'll heap sheaves of hours inside your ward
then babble about what I've learnt of mowing:
nibs and tangs and snaths, heels and toes
and edges – esoteric glossaries
for parts of tools grown rusty through disuse;
the sharpening of blades; and principles
of movement, trimming techniques, windrows, spill.
I have a hunch all this might interest you –
who drove us at weekends to run round woods,
who pointed out sea-birds, steam trains, castles –
and knowing your appreciation of the technical,
if I can communicate how vital
it is to keep the hafting angle tight,
and how though the *neigung* doesn't simply
translate it can be altered with a shim
of plywood, it might transport you for an evening
from your fixed intravenous
existence where time is marked by the sickly
drip, drip, drip of antibiotics

disrupted only by the clatter of supper
sharp at six, the tea-girl's cheery 'Cuppa?
Orange squash? Hot chocolate? Champagne?'
I hesitate to dwell too long on sharpening
the blade ... I'll paraphrase: with a quality
natural whetstone, never a *klumpat*,
make one complete pass from beard to point.
That's honing. Then there's peening:
to trick life from the scythe for years to come
tap the edge of the blade with a hammer,
tease it out like pastry ... But time is getting tight
so what I want to finish on tonight
are those principles of movement: staying true,
the simple shift of weight from foot to foot,
keeping give in the knees and judging the lean,
meditating on how we breathe
so we avoid those unexpected blips,
the woody stumps that send our pulses skittish.
Let's focus now on minimising spill
as late sun curves around the outfield,
concentrate on holding a line,
get satisfaction from a job well done,
hope that we have learnt enough to guide us
through the mass of grass as yet uncut.

The Details:
An Interview with Jan Zwicky
Jay Ruzesky

JR: You have said, 'Philosophy is thinking in love with clarity.' Can you tell me what poetry is?

JZ: Poetry is a big genus! Epic, formal verse, free verse, nursery rhymes, song lyrics – to be distinguished, at least sometimes, from lyric poetry – it's a long list! Most poetry involves rhythmically structured or patterned language, but even that (or what I'm trying to point to with that) is not true of prose poetry, which attempts to evoke the mood or emotional tone of lyric poetry while avoiding what we might call a 'singing' line. Wittgenstein would tell you that poetry is a 'family resemblance' concept: everyone in the family is related, somehow, but there's no single trait that every family member shares. (Cousin George looks like Grandad Atwater, and Maisie looks like Bill, but none of 'em looks like anybody else.)

Within that family, one of the members, lyric poetry, interests me a lot. And if it's OK to shift the focus a little, I can try to say something about lyric thought and expression (whatever the medium).

The word 'lyric' in English comes from the Greek word for lyre and so its lineage involves music. Music clearly means, but it doesn't mean the same way that language does. Music's meaning is a function of resonance and resonance involves a kind of integrity. Think of a chord. The chord is what it is because of the multiple resonant relations that its individual tones have to one another. If you remove one of the tones, or alter it just slightly – like turning an E natural into an E flat – you fundamentally change the nature of the whole. A perfectly tuned chord, we might say, is coherent. And that, I think, is the basis of what we mean by lyric thought: it's thinking in love with coherence. It seeks understanding by finding coherence, and it strives for coherence – resonant integrity – in expression.

So is lyric poetry a kind of poetry that's literally musical – sort of sing-song? Not exactly, or not always: for there are many things we describe as lyric that don't have any aural component at all. Think about Vermeer. When you hear people saying 'Vermeer's paintings are lyric...' (which they often do) what could they mean?

I'm compressing the argument here, but this is my guess: we say Vermeer's paintings (or Wittgenstein's *Tractatus*) are lyric because every detail counts. Every thing in them is resonant, every aspect is attuned to at least some other aspect. In compositions where the degree of attunement among aspects is very high, there is no real distinction between details and centres; such compositions are, we might say, radically coherent. Lyric poetry is an attempt to express lyric thought or awareness in language, and it tries to use language in a way in which every detail is resonant.

This way of thinking about lyric poetry obviates another conception of 'lyric', familiar to lots of English students: the Romantic conception of lyric poetry – poetry as quasi-confessional, poetry that exalts the individual ego. In the kind of radically coherent composition I'm interested in, you often don't get a confessional stance or a preoccupation with the self: you get a preoccupation with the world. The self as inevitable player in the whole can be present; but it's not the focus. It's there often as a gesture of humility, an acknowledgement of a perspective on the whole, but reaching toward that whole nonetheless. Is the poem about the moon, or about the finger pointing to it? In the conception of lyric I'm interested in, it turns out almost always to be about the moon.

JR: So poetry opens possibility as opposed to the way language, in a 'scientific' or objective way, does not?

JZ: Could we make another distinction here? Science itself, and the way many scientists think, is not always that different from lyric thought.

So we really do need to use the word 'scientific' in scare quotes, as you do, when we're setting up this contrast. When we use it this way, we're referring to a picture of science – one common in the media and in academic humanities departments. That picture sees science as a kind of thinking bound by rigid and simplistic canons of logic, aimed at exploiting and controlling the world. This is really, still, Francis Bacon's mid-seventeenth century conception of science.

What is the relation between lyric thought and this Baconian picture of science? I don't think lyric poetry is 'subjective' in a sense that contrasts with Baconian 'objectivity'; it's not (principally) aimed at voicing an unchallengeable, irreducibly personal view. But I do think that if you read a good lyric poem, you have to give yourself to ways of thinking that aren't conditioned by the Baconian ideal. And that allows you to acknowledge that you do know things in a way that Baconian science doesn't. Culturally, we try to control such knowing by marginalising things like lyric poetry and saying, 'Oh, the arts are about imagination, and the imagination is for making things up. What they say isn't "true"; they're not "objective".' It's all politics, that talk. It's a way to control ways of knowing that are inimical to a cultural alliance between capitalism and technology, which is part of the West's inheritance from the Enlightenment. The imagination can but doesn't always 'make things up'; in fact, imagination – which allows us to perceive likenesses and similarities – is fundamental to knowing the way things are.

JR: When we think of 'environmental literature' there are at least two aesthetic modes we might have in mind. One is the kind of writing (poetry and 'imaginative' writing) that is called Literature, and the other is any writing at all *about* the environment. In the 'literary' mode, poetry seems the most common form of expression about environmental ideas.

JZ: Hm. So you're saying we don't find as much fiction that has nature as its primary focus as we do lyric poetry? You may be right. And there's one reason that lyric poetry might be a common way of voicing our experience of the natural world. If every detail in a lyric poem manages to be in resonant relation to the whole, then the poem is a kind of ecology. This allows its structure to be enactive, to express awareness of some other ecology without distorting it. (Of course not every lyric poem is perfect! What matters is that it is a serious attempt at enactive expression; this is what it's aiming at. So the gesture is not, at root, structurally hostile to what it is trying to say.)

You go down to the marsh, say... there are the bull rushes, and there are the water striders, and there are the frogs' eggs. And there are little downy seeds in the air and they land on the surface of the water as it is cooling. All these 'details' matter to how the marsh holds together, and when we are connected to the world, breathing with the world, how we know requires a medium of expression that doesn't, in its own structural gestures, undercut our insight. The kind of knitting, the kind of coherence we experience in the marsh, and our experience of our relatedness to it, requires a non-Baconian form of expression to do it justice. On the other hand, if you think the world is a machine, then the best way to say that is with language that functions like a machine.

JR: In her review of *Lyric Philosophy* Phyllis Webb says, 'The lyric may have had its day. Why? Because of our difficulty in maintaining a coherent world view when our personal, private psyches are fractured and the world we view [is] appalling.'

JZ: This is a counsel of despair. This is to say, it's over so don't try. No, it's to say more – it's over so you *can't* try.

I revere Phyllis as a thinker and artist, and agree with her that it's over; but I think there is much beauty in the world. Even in Western European human beings, even in the midst of barbaric suffering, in the camps, on the streets. And it's overwhelmingly present in the rainforest, under the prairie sky, on the coast of Ellesmere Island, even as these ecosystems die. I understand why Phyllis says what she says, but I actually think it's wrong not to respond to beauty with love, to refuse to see because of pain. The world, even under threat of cataclysmic human-induced change, is a lyric whole; and opening ourselves to perception of this can heal our culturally fractured psyches.

JR: You say, 'It's over.' What is?

JZ: I think massive economic breakdown is coming soon. It's happening independently but it will ride on the heels of environmental degradation. Sea levels are going to rise. That's all it will take. But we also know that marine ecologies are unravelling at a staggering rate. We also know that global warming is already having serious effects on many biotas. Everywhere. We can't save them with science. We can't save them with this culture. This culture will pay the price with its death, and with the deaths of a lot of other cultures and beings, both human and non. My guess is that the cockroaches and the anaerobic bacteria are going to survive, along with the jellyfish. How much else? I don't know.

JR: That seems like thinking that could scare people into inaction. What other choice is there?

JZ: But don't we do people a disservice if we think they are – what? too ill-equipped? too immature? – to handle the truth? Death is coming to this culture and it's the kind of death that's going to be like a slow motion car accident after centuries of cultural drunk driving.

'Do what you can!' The idea of political activism is itself woven into the fabric of Enlightenment thought. Our culture is not a culture of acceptance, nor of adapting the self to the larger circumstances. It aims to adapt the circumstances to the desires of the self. This attitude is actually part of the problem. But are there alternatives in this culture? Yes, I think so. Our situation is in some ways similar to the Warring States period in China. Think of the way intellectuals and poets reacted then – they withdrew, and embraced poverty, in order to meditate on the natural world. Thomas Merton offers some striking observations on this theme. He talks (is it in *Seven Storey Mountain?*) about the sense that he has that somewhere a couple of dozen guys are praying and they're holding the whole damn thing together. It's an echo of the Hebrew notion of the Lamed-Vav Tzaddikim, the thirty-six just people. What we see in these cases is a reaction that is essentially the reaction of prayer. And by that, I don't mean 'Let's pray to God so God will make it alright.' I mean deep, reflective, meditative immersion in and compassion for what is happening. A widening of the self. There is both an acceptance of responsibility and an acknowledgement of truth in that gesture.

It's how lyric poetry can matter, if it's authentic. Praising and mourning. The praise song and the elegy are two sides of the same coin and they are annealed. We speak elegies when the thing that naturally draws praise from us is gone. It is in this praising and mourning – really experiencing what is, and what is happening – that we begin the reconstructive work of changing the culture.

And, as part of this meditative work, we recycle, and we walk or take public transit, we don't waste water, we don't waste heat – we try to act responsibly, that is, responsively toward the other beings with whom we cohabit. But we don't try to 'fix' the world. We adapt our desires to what respectful and thoughtful living allows, and in this find joy. Real joy, not some puritanical satisfaction at having 'done the right thing'. The self widens.

JR: I'd like to ask you about your assertion that the world is 'real' and is 'out there' independent of us. I wonder if the contention that the world is real and 'other' than us creates a bigger separation between people and the world. Isn't part of the problem that we see ourselves as unnatural?

JZ: Well, you know, I think many of us are unnatural. (I include myself!) Elsewhere, I've connected this issue to the notion of wilderness. Wilderness, I think, exists in greater or lesser degrees wherever we allow communities of non-humans to shape us at least as much as or more than we shape them. This is what it is for a human to be 'natural'. If you don't pay attention to the clouds and the forest, let the things you do and want be conditioned by what they do and want, you have become, to a degree, 'unnatural'. When you become more responsive, you become more 'natural'. It is also possible for a person in the midst of an intensely urban landscape to become attuned to the chrome and the glass and so become 'natural' there. But then there's the question of the relation of the chrome and the glass to the non-human world...

JR: We seem a little hopeless as a species these days. And yet we do go on. I was listening to Jean Vanier's Massey Lectures and I picked up on a line I liked very much. He says, 'The purpose of civilisation is to help us pretend that things are better than they are.'

Somehow we seem bent on seeing order in this chaos.

JZ: We have to define 'civilisation'. If we mean 'culture', it's quite clear that not only human beings possess civilisation in that sense. It's another word for ecology. When we think of human cultures, we sometimes think of stuff – artistic and intellectual efflorescences, or more recently, in this culture, technological ones. But really culture is a way of being in the world, a set of dynamic relationships.

Clearly non-humans live in cultures too. Just spend half an hour paying attention to the world 'out there'! It's not chaos: it's a succession.* Plants, animals (as well as human animals) interact, depend on, communicate and have relationships that are extended in time. The idea that only humans have culture is at the heart of an anthropocentric way of seeing. Maybe that is the quintessence of this culture: that it imagines non-humans live in a kind of chaos. This is deeply sad.

JR: That sheds new light on my question: does Nature speak or does Nature listen? Well, nature speaks, we just don't get it.

JZ: But we get enough of it to know that communication is happening, which is why there can be real, deep, interspecific relationships.

And we can get better at getting it. There are human cultures that are much more predisposed to 'get' more of it. Sustainable cultures. If you have the good fortune to be born into a sustainable human culture, chances are the natural world is speaking loudly and with complexity to you most of the time.

JR: Such a culture would hear the resonances!

JZ: Exactly, because the humans in it would be listening.

– University of Victoria, 23rd May 2008

The Quabbin

David Troupes

The enormities. The big guns of land. Wolf call of loons
for my ignorance and the long greens
of Mount Zion prostrate in its flood. The dispossessed skies,
the necessary waters. Our boat

is a flake of sun, an afterthought of tin.
Across the reservoir a dozen engines
stop. Leaves
and jays begin. The slight wind, the water-borrowed sounds
     of the hills. Hills

cup their palms and kneel. Sunlight searching the stones and
     a day-moon arriving
as my father talks
about his father
dead, how suddenly small he looked, swallowed in the white folds.
     Which

was the truer man? To what side lies the distortion? Heat.
Heat driving the piles, and we
merest puppets of summer soak our shirts and let the reservoir run
in brooks down our skin. The land in its ignorance takes us

for loons, for wolves. We are held
among the folds, the late leaving breeze, the crestings of August.
In our slightness we
are possessed. We are unnecessary.

Wonder

Julie Gabrielli

A response to Marie Howe's poem, 'Annunciation'

Read this poem aloud, or better yet, listen to the poet herself
reading it.

Even if I don't see it again — nor ever feel it
I know it is — and that if once it hailed me
it ever does —

And so it is myself I want to turn in that direction
not as towards a place, but it was a tilting
within myself,

as one turns a mirror to flash the light to where
it isn't — I was blinded like that — and swam
in what shone at me

only able to endure it by being no one and so
specifically myself I thought I'd die
from being loved like that.

Hearing this poem for the first time made me cry.

A single poem of ninety-six words elicits the same response as the event itself.

How is that possible?

STANZA 1: It hailed me

Steering into the wind and crashing down the waves is utterly consuming, the word *afraid* no match for what I am feeling. Wrenched from all that I know, I am beyond fear, beyond any nameable emotion. I focus on my job, immersed in the drama, the surreal darkness in daytime, the deafening wind, the cold rain and spray, the extreme motion of the boat as the bow slams repeatedly into the water. I keep doing my job, staying focused.

And then.

We break free of time. The storm raises its skirts to reveal a luminous yellow glow around the entire horizon. The wind and rain halt. I shimmer with energy, suffused in glowing calm, full, complete, in oneness with all. The world, not just the bay, is entirely round with me in it, a tiny crab in the palm of a vast hand.

So integral a part of it, no longer in my body, I *am* the bay, the sky, the world, the golden light; I am all of it and none of it. I begin to weep with joy. The electric charge in my body hums on and on, bathing me in love.

STANZA 2: Tilting within myself

Events like this defy attempts to describe them. This is not a topic that can be known, analysed, picked apart, turned into a neat story. Believe me, I have tried. How does one net a liquid living light, or know the energy that drives the universe? It doesn't want me to tell stories. It wants me to let go and be ravished.

Hildegaard von Bingen wrote words, drew pictures, composed music, ran a monastery, and practiced botany and medicine over a lifetime. That's how much horsepower she brought to bear on this energy. She called it God.

We need these reminders. We need them in art and we need them in life. Speaking about her work, Marie Howe said, 'Art holds the knowledge that we are both living and dying at the same time.' From a private expressive impulse, a poem becomes a shared experience, a connection between two people who have never met. And a connection to the shimmering magic of this world.

Marie Howe's poem happened when she let go of certainty. Acting on a suggestion (one might say a dare) from her long-time friend, poet Stanley Kunitz, she made several attempts and threw them away. She gave up. Her will finally exhausted, another voice came through.

Her poem is an anthem to the great mystery as well as a doorway into it. I sometimes fantasise about skipping all the struggle and resistance of the creative process and going straight to the giving-over part. It does seem to be a package deal, though. The will is a sentinel with the job of preparing you to cross the threshold. Entry is barred until you are sufficiently humbled. You must appreciate your limitations and give up the need for control and certainty. You must choose to resist no longer.

STANZA 3: I was blinded like that

I want to make the case that this poem – all poetry and all art – arises from the luminous wholeness behind the broken world we inhabit. A poem or a painting may or may not be an attempt to reveal this wholeness. Through attention, presence and noticing, the artist courts a relationship with the material of the everyday. A poet may seek to describe something quite ordinary, like the sound of rain falling on leaves. A simple painting of a sunrise over water, made for the sheer joy of looking, might just stumble into a glimpse of transcendence.

Touching other realities has always been part of human experience. Modern Western culture belittles and denies dimensions that cannot be quantified, measured, and named. One could argue, as Barbara Ehrenreich does, that it's just as unscientific to ignore and discount mystical experiences as it is to ascribe transcendent or numinous meaning to them. She writes that by distancing ourselves from the sacred we have become far lonelier than we need to be.

Still, we live by this story that the human species has evolved past the need for magic and mystery. By this logic, then, poetry, art, music, drama – all creative endeavours – are unnecessary, or at best decoration and entertainment. And yet the world keeps throwing big events at us: hurricanes, bombings, refugee crises, economic collapse, social upheaval. Confusion and chaos can pop up anywhere at any time. We don't have answers. We aren't in control.

Marie Howe's poem is an invitation to a state of awe. We moderns are sorely awe-deprived from our long commutes; hours in front of computer screens; drills, memorisation and standardised testing in schools; and our general getting-ahead focus. We are disconnected – from other people and from the wider community of *life*.

It is easier to slip between worlds when we are removed from our human-made environment and stripped of the technologies of distraction. Vision quests rely on the energies and histories of certain landscapes for their potency. Ms. Ehrenreich was hiking in a California landscape, all rolling hills and sunlight and vistas. Aldous Huxley allied with the botanical guide mescaline to travel to his otherworld. My own doorway took the form of a full-body, multi-sensory immersion into the teeth of a gale while on a small sailboat.

STANZA 4: Being no-one

The very act of making art or writing poetry courts the numinous. Pay close attention, listen inside, engage all the senses. I imagine that Marie Howe summoned all of herself, brought her history, skill, experience, intelligence, belief and scepticism to bear in the attempt to express something true. And then she let go and stopped trying.

I am drawn to poetry with last lines that pack a punch. Rilke's 'Archaic Torso of Apollo' ends with, 'You must change your life.' Rumi counsels the reader to 'Say yes quickly.' David Wagoner's 'Lost' advises, 'Stand still. The forest knows / Where you are. You must let it find you.'

The end of 'Annunciation' hurts. It is bewildering and honest and exhilarating and true as only a poem can be.

Events that challenge our standard ways of relating to the world are not meant to be reassuring. But they are important lessons in how to live. How to live now, while things are (mostly) steady. And how to live when they are not.

Shown my unquestioning acceptance of the illusion of separation, the puny story of human supremacy, I never again doubted the existence of this other, vast and fiercely loving reality. I have also rarely known what to do about it. The event has defied telling, because it is more of a feeling than a story.

That doesn't stop me from trying. If I have to write and paint my way back to the wholeness that hides behind the world, I will. I still don't know to what end I am so motivated, and even that's the point. There is no end, there is only now and now and these reminders of the energies of love and wonder.

Four Poets' Houses

Paul Kingsnorth

1. Dove Cottage, Grasmere, England

Until now, poetry has meant nothing to me. I've never understood it, or much cared. Most of the other stuff I've been forced to read in Mr Mitchell's sixth form English class has been suicidally tedious. Alexander Pope's verbose dribblings. Jane Austen's yawnsome bonnets and carriage rides. What was it with the eighteenth century? Was *everybody* boring, or just the ones who wrote books?

Now we're doing Wordsworth. I've heard of him, of course: he wrote a poem about daffodils. Now I have to read something called *Tintern Abbey*, which is far longer than any poem should ever be, and is about some stones that used to be an Abbey. I fear the worst.

It isn't about the Abbey, though, not really. It's about a man who loves nature, and who is trying to put that love into words. And even though those words include 'sylvan' and 'perchance' and 'wilt thou' and 'hither', somehow I get this straight away. 'Nature never did betray the heart that loved her,' says William, and I agree, I feel the same, but I'm too embarrassed to tell anyone I know. I've been up on the same mountains as this man, and I've experienced, like him, 'A motion and a spirit, that impels / All thinking things, all objects of all thought, / And rolls through all things.' He gets it, even from two hundred years in the past.

Wordsworth was my first poetic love, and you always remember your first love. He was a Romantic and so am I, and Romanticism, as I later discovered, was not a floppy-wristed affectation for people who prefer flowers to football, but a radical proposition. Freshly returned from a stint in revolutionary France during which, as a supporter of the revolution, he narrowly escaped death, Wordsworth took up residence near his friend Samuel Coleridge in a tiny peasant's cottage in the Cumberland village of Grasmere, and began composing poems which would be thrown like bombs at the orthodoxies of rationalism, humanism, progress and empire. *Lyrical Ballads,* Wordsworth and Coleridge's first book together, contains an introduction which reads like a manifesto for both poetry and life: against the machine, for the human heart and spirit. With the industrial revolution beginning to turn the world upside down, this stuff must have felt dangerous.

I didn't visit Dove Cottage until years after I first read Wordsworth, by which time it had long since stopped feeling dangerous. These days, the poet's old house is one of the north of England's major tourist attractions. Grasmere has been broadsided by a vast car park designed to accommodate the coach tours which pour into the cottage every five minutes, to take the guided tours around the tiny rooms. After your tour, there are some fetching Wordsworth postcards and pens and mugs and notebooks which you can buy in the attached gift shop. Or you can wander into the village and visit one of the many boutiques, cafes, hotels and fudge shops named after the poet. You can also visit his grave, which has daffodils planted on it. Everyone knows the poem about daffodils. The first bit, at least.

Once this little place was a den of hallucinogens and radical notions, of outsiders and freaks and rebels against the future. But that kind of thing is achingly old-fashioned now. The machine has outlasted it, because the machine can package and sell you anything, including hallucinogenic poems written by freaks and rebels. Romanticism is no longer threatening, but it does a very nice line in tea towels.

2. The Boathouse, Laugharne, Wales

Dylan Thomas has never interested me much. Writing this essay, I realised I don't even have any of his books on my shelf. Why do some writers connect with you and others just sail past? Nobody knows, and it probably doesn't matter. When I read Thomas, I can admire what he did with language at the same time as being unmoved by his message. Perhaps that's because he didn't have a message. Perhaps I'm the sort of person who needs messages, and perhaps that isn't good. But who makes the rules here? Is it me? I suppose it must be.

The boathouse, though, is another matter. A tiny wooden shed nestled under a cliff on the edge of the astonishing Taf estuary in south Wales, the view from the window is wonderful. There is space, air, water, freedom. I visited it when I was a student, and I thought that this was exactly the kind of place a poet should write in. Everything made of wood, and whisky bottles on the desk, and prints pinned up at angles on the walls and nothing in view from the window but sand and sky and wheeling gulls. I wanted to be a poet myself by this point: in fact, I already was. I had a folder crammed with execrable sub-Larkin verse in my small student room. One day, I was going to work in a shed like this. Maybe I would drink myself to death too, like Thomas did, just to show I was the real thing. That hasn't happened yet, but there's still time.

You can still visit the boathouse. It's very popular. People remember that poem Dylan wrote about his dad dying. Like Dove Cottage, the boathouse now has a nice little tearoom attached. It doesn't do whisky, though. It doesn't have a licence.

3. Casa de Isla Negra, Isla Negra, Chile

This does not count. This should not even be on the list. Really, this is not right.

Casa de Isla Negra is one of Pablo Neruda's three large houses. He designed it himself, in the shape of a ship. It sits on a cliff overlooking an azure sea. Neruda was a collector, and the house is filled with beautiful collections: ships' figureheads, glasses and ceramics, paintings, ships in bottles, seashells (a whole room is dedicated to these). There are huge stone fireplaces, still stained black with soot, and balconies designed to look like the crows' nests of ships. Every space is crammed with something elegant and interesting and expensive, and though everything is unique, it all somehow fits together.

This is not a poet's house. It is a politician's house, a diplomat's house, a socialite's house, the house of a man who was high up in the Chilean political establishment and who, had he not died soon after Pinochet's 1973 coup – murdered, it now seems likely, by the new dictator – would have led Chile's government-in-exile. Instead, he is buried outside, with his wife, overlooking the sea. Given all that, it seems churlish to complain. It seems petty.

Still, I can't help it: a poet should not have a house like this. And he certainly shouldn't have three of them. Perhaps you will put this down to envy, and if you did, you would be right. Not only is this house in a beautiful place, but it is filled with beautiful things. I would love to have a house like this; I would love to be the sort of person who could create a house like this, but I know I'm not. Even if I had the money, I wouldn't have the breeding or the style or the panache or the self-belief.

But let's not lose track of the problem, for there is a high literary principle at stake here. Poets should live – and, ideally, die – in garrets like Chatterton, or in little dark cottages like Wordsworth, or in whisky-sodden boatsheds like Thomas, or in locked bedrooms like

Emily Dickinson. They should not live in palatial seaside mansions crammed with expensive antiques. It is not right.

There's a great passage in Geoff Dyer's book about D.H. Lawrence, *Out of Sheer Rage,* in which he finds himself in the well-appointed London street where the novelist Julian Barnes lives. 'I knew,' he writes, 'that in one of these large, comfortable houses Julian Barnes was sitting at his desk, working, as he did every day. It seemed an intolerable waste of a life, *of a writer's life especially,* to sit at a desk in this nice, dull street in north London. It seemed, curiously, a betrayal of the idea of the writer.'

The idea of the writer: that's the thing. Writers, and especially poets, are supposed to sit outside the world and look in. They are not supposed to run the place. They have to be outsiders. They have to be hungry and uninterested in worldly success. They have to be poor, or at least not rich, because if they become rich they become fat and complacent and then they have nothing to say.

Neruda, presumably, would not agree with any of this. Unlike me, he was no Romantic. He was a communist, a supporter of Castro and Stalin, and he believed in the social and political obligations of writers. 'Come and see the blood in the streets', he famously demanded. Yet he also believed in having three houses, and in owning beautiful wine glasses and in the wonderful views of the sea from his large terrace. There is a clear contradiction here. But perhaps there is a clear contradiction at the heart of poetry; perhaps this is where it comes from. Show me the man who doesn't betray himself, and I will show you the man who can't write.

4. Thoor Ballylee, County Galway, Ireland

Forty minutes drive from where I live in the west of Ireland is the former home of Ireland's greatest ever poet, W. B. Yeats. As a building, it perfectly represents both his poetic ideals and his political prejudices. Thoor Ballylee – the poet himself named it, the word 'Thoor' being a variant on the Irish for 'tower' – is an old square Norman tower, of the kind that were built in their hundreds across this country in the early Middle Ages. Attached to the tower is a low, traditional thatched Irish cottage. They both nestle next to a stream by a beautiful arched stone bridge in a valley that even today seems out of time. Since Yeats's death in 1939, his country has changed almost beyond recognition, but this valley, and this building, have mostly survived the onslaught.

Yeats, like all great poets, never really lived in anybody else's version of accepted reality. His ideal Ireland was already past by the time he was born ('Romantic Ireland's dead and gone', he wrote in 1915, even before the Easter Rising a year later), and he found its whispers and echoes in old towers and thatched cottages, in hedges and *boreens*, in the dying faerie lore and in the mystical practices which he took seriously, and from which he drew much of his poetic strength.

Close to Thoor Ballylee is the Lady Gregory Museum, in the village of Kiltartan. Lady Gregory was Yeats' aristocratic patron. The museum is now run by an old nun who remembers the poet from when she was a child. He used to walk down the streets of Gort, she says, in a long flowing cloak, muttering poetry to himself, oblivious to those around him. Once he was coming down the stairs in Lady Gregory's grand house at nearby Coole Park, when he met a small boy on his way up. 'Hello little boy,' said the poet, his mind on greater things, 'and who might you be?' 'I'm your son,' the boy replied.

Yeats, like Wordsworth, was a Romantic. He was also a feudalist.

He believed there was true nobility both in the peasantry and in the aristocracy, and Thoor Ballylee symbolically joins both of these classes together: the castle and the cottage represent the twin pillars of his ideal Ireland. The class that Yeats despised, and which he predicted would destroy his country, was the commercial bourgeoisie. It took them a while to get going, but his prediction has been largely fulfilled. Sixty years after his death, the phenomena known as the 'Celtic Tiger' erupted across the landscape, scattering it with ugly new-build McMansions and motorways and superstores and the headquarters of Google and Facebook. By the time the bubble burst, Ireland had a quarter of a million unwanted and uninhabited houses scattered randomly across the landscape which the poet had once hymned. Many of them are now rotting away, back into the fields, their cheap concrete weeping, their plastic fascias collapsing onto the dirty gravel. The valley in which Thoor Ballylee sits is one of the few places in rural Ireland from which a new-build concrete house cannot be seen. Yeats might have been pleased at that, if nothing else.

*

Four houses in four countries. Four poets. Four ways of longing for a world that is no longer there, or which never was there, or which may one day be here but for now is still far away. Four approaches to constructing a scaffold made of words which attempts to contain the world but always fails. There are as many scaffolds as there are poets, writers, human beings.

I think I could spend a lifetime visiting poets' houses, with or without the tearooms. I think now of others I would like to see: Robinson Jeffers' magnificent Tor House, self-built on what were once the wild cliffs of Northern California, now the centre of yet another soul-destroying American suburb. The house of Emily Dickinson's parents, where she spent most of her brief life in the upstairs bedroom, looking out of the window and cramming poems into her drawers. R. S. Thomas's low, ancient cottage, built into the stone of the Lleyn peninsular in North Wales, as bleak as the man and his verse. W. S. Merwin's Hawaiian plantation of rare palms. Perhaps I could do a world tour. If only poetry paid better.

Or perhaps this is all wrong. Fossilising buildings, attaching tearooms and gift shops, taking the easiest and the fluffiest and the rhymiest bits of the poems and putting them on postcards, smoothing out the contradictions. When poetry is true it comes from a deep and ancient place. It is not for sale, really. Why preserve the building? Why build up a reputation? The poet is dead, the poems are still here. Do we need to see the poet's whisky bottle on the poet's table? Yes, it interests us: but do we need to see it?

When Yeats first found Thoor Ballylee it was a ruin, like so many other Norman towers across Ireland. He restored it, and when it was finished he inscribed a poem on a slate that he had fixed to the tower's outside wall. The poem described how he had restored the tower for his wife, using materials from the local landscape. But it was also written in the expectation that one day the place would return to its previous state. 'And may these characters remain,' it ends, 'when all is ruin once again.'

It costs a lot of money to install fire doors and attach a tearoom. It costs little or nothing to get hold of a second-hand book of poems. A true poem, unlike a house, can't be fossilised. If it contains truth or beauty, it will always contain them. It will outlast brick and stone. We should hope so, anyway.

Nine Nests:
Lessons for Spring

Tom Pow

THE FIRST NEST

We sit opposite each other at a lone table high in the forest canopy.
The sympathetic waiter has drifted behind one of the larger trees to
keep an eye out for wolves and to dream of Prague. There are two
glasses of water before us, each catches the light sifting through the
tree's crown. Idly, we make a nest from the most obvious materials
to hand: the thick twigs of statement and circumstance; bound with
the ready-made narratives of memory. We lean towards each other,
with each weave becoming more absorbed in our task. Intimacy is
delicate work: spider-silk, saliva, moss. Each move invites a counter-
move – our nest is a dance and the dance is trust. Once upon an
island, you were a barefoot girl, brought up by a grandmother
whose death still makes you cry. She brought you to a churchyard,
where, shaded from the fierce sun, a marble Madonna stood, gentle
and serene, hands held out to the world. How could she be left
empty-handed? In a quiet hour, like this one, at the day's end, as
now, you placed an old nest on her open palms. As you tell me this,
I plait your story into the nest we have made. I am shoulder to
shoulder with you, within the green shadow of your silence, the
leaves whispering of the sea. Our nest hovers over an altar of water
and light. Madonna of the Nest, give sustenance to the poet and to

the mother she will become. And this, above all: Let her be the disciple of what she alone chooses to enact.

THE SECOND NEST

This bird builds its nest in garden hedges, in laurel bushes, rhododendron or in any common garden tree. Perhaps an apple tree or a pear tree or a plum tree. Perhaps a cherry tree, a medlar, an ornamental fir. It's a bird that likes to be around us; so, it seems apt that, if you were to hold your hands in the form of a boat, the bird could settle snugly there. It comes to your bird table for bread soaked in milk, for pieces of apple, for any fatty scraps. It reminds you, with a few scattered pecks, your fruit is ripe for picking. It sings its heart out in spring. In short, it delights you. There is no difficulty for this bird in finding material to build its nest – there is ample from the garden cuttings of suburbia: twigs, hedge clippings, soft, young hair eased from a brush and gifted to the breeze. The eggs – two, three or four – shine at you, like eyes, from the depth of the hedge or from the tree you have climbed. This bird's salvation does not rest in obfuscation. Finding its nest is no mystery. That lies elsewhere. At such times as when, in your bed at night, you go over the day's bullying or that moment when you heard your parents argue and entered, unannounced, their dry silence. So, where is your place in the world? You recall how, earlier that day, gently, you lifted branch and leaf cover to find a bird sitting, quivering in its own cavern of shredded light. It is there now, but in darkness, yet so close to where you are, bound in your tangled sheets, you can almost reach out a trembling hand to touch it. Be calm, the nest is of another world, but one you will surely enter.

THE THIRD NEST

And some birds build their nests in the hatchings of the past. It is dark back there, but the darkness creates its own light. There was a boy, many years ago now, whose neighbour found him interfering with a nest. He brought it to the attention of the boy's father. 'So, it'll be all right to leather him, if he does it again?' the neighbour said. 'Oh, yes,' said the boy's father. From that day forth, the poor boy pulled his hand back from darkness, just at the point where darkness takes on the black sheen of light.

THE FOURTH NEST

This little bird builds its nest in the most secretive places. You need to be alert to come across its nest on the lowest branches of a bush or, as here, tucked in the corner of a garden hut. A family, downsizing after their children have left home, has moved away. Their house hasn't yet sold. Or perhaps they were advised there was a higher bid in the offing. The garden tools have been taken, the old paint tins thrown out. But still the empty hut, in summer, has the smell of turned over earth and the sharp pheromones of early sexual experiment. It's a different matter in winter – it would take the harshest winter and the greatest ill-luck for someone to seek shelter in it then. But each of us knows, in these harsh times, there is such luck and there are such people. It's a simple cup nest, made of twigs mostly. But this inventive bird will use whatever else is to hand to strengthen the form – pieces of string or twine, for example; the kind that might have kept an old coat closed against the chill. The nest is lined with dried grasses, with flower-heads, spider-silk and with an abundant and welcome supply of dry grey hair. Although it may share a characteristic appearance with the common sparrow, this bird shares none of a sparrow's sociability. It remains a solitary creature, keeping itself to itself. It shrugs across the overgrown garden and builds its nest in the shadows, more in hope than in expectation. Yet if, in spring, it should be blessed with two or three eggs, small and unspectacular as itself, you would find its devotion to the clutch is nothing short of remarkable.

On the other hand, this combative little bird is a risk taker. It likes to build its nest in challenging places. Nests have been found, for example, between the rails on the west coast mainline and wedged between the cables of the Forth Road Bridge. Of course, there is danger there. But the bird, we must assume, has made a calculation between danger and the possibility of discovery – for who would think to look for a nest in such places? Evolution has equipped our intrepid adventurer with a tool suitable for the materials with which it must work. Its short, blunt, bodkin beak can bend wire and break gravel. No one would claim either it or its nest were pretty creations, but we cannot help admiring ingenuity and tenacity. For all the unwelcome pressures of the environments in which it makes its home, when the bird is held, for the purposes of ringing, its heartbeat remains steady. For, after all, your hands are the least of the dangers it has faced. Its eggs are a metallic grey, dotted with rust. Sometimes, it is the crashing sound of the southern sleeper that causes them to hatch. There is the diminishing sound of the speeding train. Then, in the stillness which follows it, three small guttural chirpings, that, in intent, suggest a muffled swearing; of the kind you might hear directed at yet another bloody 'Suicide Johnny', lying flayed on the track. Let the trains go, says the media star with the face of a crushed crepe. Why should everything be held up for the sake of one selfish unfortunate? So, his wife kicked him out of the nest ... So, he'll never see his children ... Only as the train approaches the thin shanty-town lights on the outskirts of the city, does crepe-face feel appetite quell his irritation.

THE SIXTH NEST

Only the hardiest walker will come across the nest of this highland bird. And only ones with the sharpest eyes. For this diminutive bird is blessed with the art of camouflage. You've been walking for a good three hours, walking for one, climbing for two. For these two, you've been following a small burn, following it from the loch side. At times you've had to deviate, where the path grew muddy; where a clump of hazels was too dense. You arrive at a small waterfall – it's been in your sights for a good half hour! Below it, there is a clear, cool pool. You sit on a rock and tip your face to the sun. The stillness seems immense. You have grown impossibly young. As has your father. It's as if you've both climbed back through the decades to this place where understanding between you is complete. So, you guddle in the pool, while he sits above you, big as the mountain, the sun on his shoulder. Then there is just the smell of him – familiar notes of peat-smoke; leathery and sweet. You are aware of a fierce concentration of energy. A pulse. The bird is tiny, but it seems to be everywhere, on the stones above the waterfall, on its heather banks, on the branch of the hazel opposite you. Its light chirrup is the only sound you can hear, above the breathing of the wind, throughout the glacial glen. What is the bird saying? It is saying, *Is my nest built on stone, water or wood? Stone, water or wood?* Be careful as you climb and, as you climb, purify your mind with this question, *Is my nest built on stone, water or wood?* I'll wait for your return to give the answer.

THE SEVENTH NEST

For many years it was not thought possible that any bird could live up there, so high above the tree line. What would it feed on? How would its heart not freeze? These questions, and many others, still pertain. Especially, as the light there is so strong, it has not been possible to retain a satisfactory image of the nest, beyond a certain coagulation of light itself. But those who have seen them – a handful of exhausted mountaineers you might think given to such visions were it not that their reports have been so compatible – claim they are exquisite creations. Slipper-like in form, they hang from the frozen air. They appear to be woven, not composed of compacted snow as one might have expected. However, they are lined with snow, gobs of it, smoothed with a feathered breast till it is silken. Those who have been drawn to the nests comment, without exception, that they emit a blue-hued light, like lanterns. Its source must be the material out of which they are woven. Whatever that is, it is of the utmost delicacy; for, in the early days, when any one of the nests was brought down from the heights, all of it disintegrated so completely that there was nothing left of it at all. Even if one damp spot was saved, it was of such purity, the scientists averred, that it was corrupted by whatever it had touched – a glove, a container, a breath – so as to appear to have no substance that could be called its own. Still, elusiveness has done nothing but strengthen belief. The visionaries tell us, we are not designed to find these birds. Their nests should stay wherever they happen to be found.

THE EIGHTH NEST

There are, nevertheless, birds that prefer not to build their own nests, but to make use of what's there. There's nothing to distinguish these birds from others – after all, the construction of a nest involves no more than a beak, a claw, the insistent pressing and moulding of a breast. This bird makes use of these too. It has to, for most nests are built for short-term use; to service a season. Even those built with great care will, after a winter, inclement and cold, require attention. The bird for this work can adapt itself to the garden, the forest, the scrub. It travels light, but with the armoury it needs. It assesses the damage and sets about collecting the few buttressing pieces of twig required. Then it's a question of fresh bedding – out with the old moss, in with the new. To what else is left of the life that was, this vagrant bird gives no thought. And of the bird that abandoned its nest, what of it? Though it may skirt the old nest in the forest, its interest is in new thresholds, in remaking the world each spring. Yet there are others – a subset within a species – whose flight path leads them unerringly back to their primal nest. The return is rarely a contented one. It finds its former home in a sorry state: broken, shapeless, infested with bacteria and bugs. It hangs around once frequented places, hoping to pick up the odd scrap of news; to be enveloped by old, familiar rhythms. But soon it learns the migrant cannot return; the world is not as it once was. All other birds know this, know that it's the next tree, the next happy bush that will house their nest. I feel for the bird that, between seasons, feels the pull of its past, its own fulsomeness weighing it down; as I feel for the other bird that asks – as we would of a village, a city, a town – 'Was it as beautiful as memory paints it?'

THE NINTH NEST

When autumn is at its end and all the leaves have fallen, we shall see whether or not we were right. We followed the flight of the birds; we listened to their songs. But, before we saw the black discs of their nests, held in these bare forks, we couldn't be fully sure. How naked they look in their uselessness. Yet there is also something brazen about the way they decorate that tree with a memory of instinctual life. The birds are all away, doing what birds do, and we are here, staring at emptiness, longing to be seduced by the invisible.

Windfall plums:
a few words about haiku

Robert Alcock

I.

Last summer, out of the blue, I started writing haiku again.

It began, auspiciously enough, at a Zen monastery. I had gone with my family to a week-long retreat at Plum Village, the centre near Bergerac, France, founded by Vietnamese Buddhist monk and poet Thich Nhat Hanh. Something in the way the buildings stood their ground, the stylistic fusion of east and west, recalled my long-lost California of childhood holidays at my grandparents' house near Monterey, set amid redwoods and live oaks. With no distractions, real-life or electronic, and feeling no particular call from the Dharma teachings on offer, I spent the week mostly just wandering about, without any real aim except to practice the art of just happening to be in the right place at the right time, and to record what I found there. Life was suddenly vast, empty, and hopeful. And into this space poems began to fall like – well, like windfall plums.

> rain on the roof
> of the meditation hall –
> did i zip my tent?
>
> Plum Village

> by the zen garden
> i taste the monks' stash
> of hot sauce
>
> Plum Village

2.

My first flirtation with haiku was twenty years ago now. I knew very little about the form, but it attracted me for reasons that were as much practical as philosophical. I was on an extended tour by bike in the American southwest, from Colorado to California, and needed something to occupy my mind as I was riding. Haiku were short and simple enough to compose and revise in my head during the long empty miles. My haiku were pretty rough around the edges, though genuine and from the heart, but one of them later won a prize which paid for the trip: £500 for a two-line, seven-word poem – probably the best rate of pay per word I'm likely to receive in my life. Of course you could call it a fluke, and perhaps it was; but I took it as a hint that a life of integrity might, in fact, be a viable proposition. I'd gone on the bike ride and written those haiku just for their own sake, and now here I was getting paid for it.

Needless to say, no lucrative lifestyle beckoned as a haiku poet (nor any other kind, for that matter). In fact winning the award was a serious blow to my writing, since for years afterwards I judged whatever I wrote by the arbitrary standard of that one success. Still, I continued to come up with the occasional haiku while doing my best to live a life of integrity. I hope I can say I'm still fighting to a draw on that one.

in the desert
there is no soundtrack

Hopiland, October 1996[1]

3.

Haiku is, or are, probably the most misapprehended of all major poetic forms. Every literate person more or less knows what makes a sonnet a sonnet or a limerick a limerick, but the only thing everyone 'knows' about haiku – that it's a Japanese poem in three lines with five, seven, and five syllables – tells you nothing meaningful about the form. In Japanese, haiku are normally written on one line rather than three[2] and don't necessarily conform to the 5–7–5 rule.[3] And over the past fifty years the form has transcended its Japanese origins via an explosion of haiku in other languages, including, of course, English, in which a syllable can be as short as 'a' or as long as 'strength'. Most English-language haiku are either very flexible with the syllable rule or else ignore it completely; many have three lines, but there are plenty with only one, or two, or even four. As befits its Zen roots, haiku is a formless form. It's not form but spirit that makes it haiku. There is no better expression of this spirit – nor, I think, of the 'uncivilised' writing championed by Dark Mountain – than that given by Basho himself:

> Go to the pine if you want to learn about the pine, or to the bamboo if you want to learn about the bamboo. And in doing so, you must leave your subjective preoccupation with yourself. Otherwise you impose yourself on the object and do not learn. Your poetry issues of its own accord when you and the object have become one – when you have plunged deep enough into the object to see something like a hidden glimmering there.[4]

In spirit, haiku is universal. An Irish monk of the ninth century scribbles in the margin of a sacred manuscript:

How lovely it is today!
The sunlight breaks and flickers
on the margin of my book.

translated from the Irish by Thomas Kinsella[5]

The manuscript is doubly illuminated, and so are we.

4.

But you'll look in vain for haiku in most collections of English-language poetry, aside from dedicated haiku publications that preach to the converted. You're more likely to find pseudo-haiku or meta-haiku: light verse that apes, mocks, or comments on the form of haiku, diligently counting syllables as it goes, while mostly ignoring the spirit. One meta-haiku by Adrian Mitchell might stand for the whole:

Haiku? Too easy.
Everyone knows poetry
Should be difficult.

from *Blue Coffee, Poems 1985–1996*

If 'writing free verse is like playing tennis with the net down',[6] then haiku – once you quit counting syllables like a dutiful child – is like playing tennis with no net, ball, racket or court; in fact, nothing to show the onlooker that you are actually playing a game rather than just standing in a field. Nothing to cling to; nothing to get a handle on. Who would watch a game like that? No surprise, then, if haiku makes people antsy, especially the people whose job it is to judge, edit and compile poetry. Simon Armitage, introducing his anthology of short poems, writes, 'I felt a strong obligation to include at least one haiku, and for that reason have not done so.'[7] Well, quite.

As the poetry teacher says in Chang-dong Lee's sublime film, *Poetry*: 'It is not difficult to write a poem; what's difficult is to have the heart to write it.'

5.
The remarkable thing about my summer was that the still space which had opened up – still and empty despite being full of frogs, dragonflies, sunflowers and crescent moons – stayed open for far longer than it had any right to. We returned home, and became immersed in household routine; we went on holiday to the south of Spain, to the beach and the mountains, and came back again; the harvest season heaped us with a glut of tomatoes, squash, windfall apples and plums. And during it all I seemed still to be passing through one real live moment after another, living in each one in turn. I don't mean that I was aware of living *every* moment of every day – that would be too much – but still, there was no end of moments, all clamouring to be recorded and become part of my personal mythology of time. During the summer I wrote, oh, a couple of hundred haiku, I suppose. As to whether they are of any literary merit, or have a true haiku spirit – I can't say, and in any case I'm hardly the one to judge.

> by the woodpile,
> last winter remembering
> next winter

> Voto, Cantabria, August 2015

dusk:
swifts swoop low
over the motorway

Castilla-La Mancha

redhanded –
stealing
a mulberry

Las Alpujarras, Granada

late camp –
only the moon's
wry smile

Las Alpujarras, Granada

at the zoo,
girl picks blackberries
through a chainlink fence

Cabarceno, Cantabria

6.

Not until the autumn did the space begin to close. The children started new schools; we moved into a flat in town (temporarily, as it turned out); the many teeth of civilisation – street grids, traffic, noise, newspapers, work, paperwork, shopping, timetables, grades and constant electronic distraction – began to grind me down. I gradually stopped writing haiku and became mildly depressed. That was nothing new, but now I was conscious, more than ever, that what I had always called depression was really just another name for the all-pervading *re*pression of the Machine. I still keep that awareness, the harvest of last summer.

> pavement wet –
>
> from her umbrella drops
>
> small change

Laredo, Cantabria, September 2015

Notes

1. still haiku award, autumn 1998. Published in *still, a journal of short verse*
2. 'On translating haiku in one line' by Hiroaki Sato. From *Right under the big sky, I don't wear a hat. The haiku and prose of Hosai Ozaki.* (Stone Bridge Press, 1993).
3. For example, Basho's seminal 'autumn crow' haiku, which consists of nineteen or twenty syllables in different versions.
4. Basho, *The Narrow Road to the Deep North and other travel sketches,* translated and with and introduction by Nobuyuki Yuasa (Penguin, 1966).
5. From *The New Oxford Book of Irish Verse,* ed. Thomas Kinsella (Oxford University Press, 1986).
6. Robert Frost, in a speech given May 17, 1935.
7. *Short and Sweet: 101 very short poems,* ed. Simon Armitage (Faber and Faber, 1999).

Third World

Mourid Barghouti

The magnet said to the iron filings:
you are totally
free
to go in whatever direction you want.

عالم ثالث

قال المغناطيس ليرادة الحديد:
أنتِ حُرّةٌ تماماً
في الاتجاه إلى حيث ترغبين!

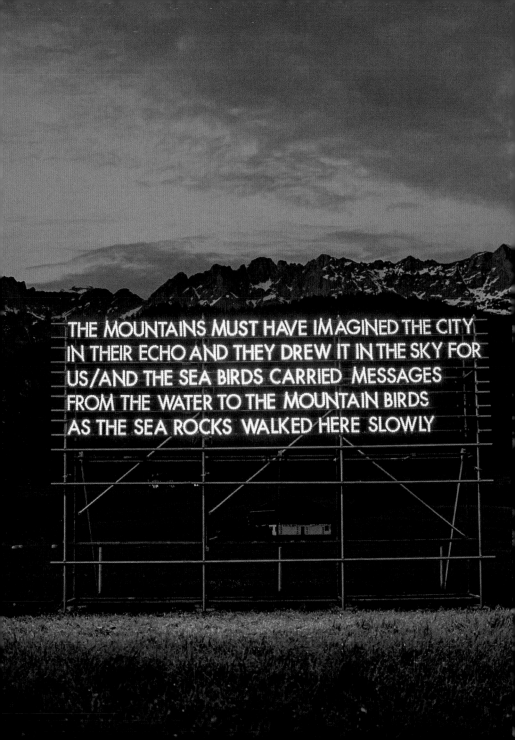

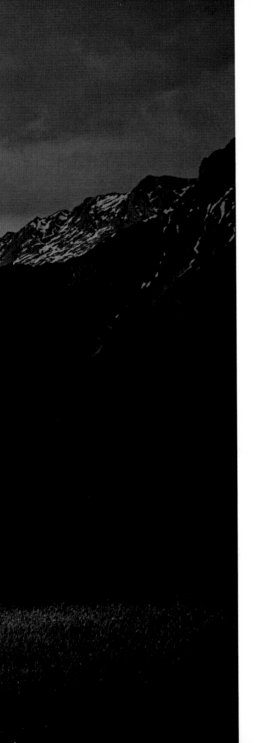

ROBERT MONTGOMERY
[previous page] Ostend Wall Piece, 2016
courtesy of the artist and Crystal Ship Festival

Leogang Poem, Austrian Alps, 2015
Light installation (photo: Mik Freud)

'To encounter the work of Robert Montgomery
is to make a tender encounter whose tenderness
is enhanced by the public, communal quality of
his work. To encounter his work is to have your
body filled with a sad thunder and your head
filled with a sad light. He is a complete artist
and works in language, light, paper, space.
He engages completely with the urban world
with a translucent poetry. His work arrives
at us through a kind of lucid social violence.
No one has blended language, form and
light in such a direct way.'
   – Dane Weatherman, Black & Blue Journal

ANDREW MAIZE Going, Going

Engraved granite stone set in the intertidal zone at Cape Split, Nova Scotia, Canada

The text from Phillip Larkin's poem 'Going, Going' is engraved on a 600 pound granite stone for the Uncommon Common Art Project. The stone was placed on the intertidal zone of Cape Split, a headland in the Bay of Fundy, home of the highest recorded tides in the world, up to 16.3 metres (53.5 feet). It lies next to an abandoned fisherman's wharf that was severely damaged by a storm last winter.

[Photos: Scott Olszowiec]

PATRIK QVIST Evig Tillväxt (Eternal Growth)
Plastic cups in chain link fence

Installed between the Stockholm School of Economics and Stockholm Public Library in March 2016, the translated text reads: Fairytales of eternal growth – other stories. Typically, my words on fences get noticed by a handful of people before they are duly removed by whoever is in charge of the particular stretch of fence. This piece was picked up by some high profile Instagram users and was shared extensively before its removal. While most of the response on social media was positive, there were some critical voices too. Qvist is 'out of touch with reality' tweeted a professor at the School of Economics – an intriguing reaction which deserves a future rendering on a fence nearby.

AUDREY DIMOLA Compass Project
New York, USA
The Compass Project was started in 2012 to undercut traditional narratives of validation and access in the art and literary worlds – no gatekeepers, no rules, no rejection, no waiting – just my words stuck up in the world on DIY printed stickers, without any indication of who would receive them or how long they would last. This experiment in ephemerality has been a source of infinite surprise and fulfillment. Strangers have become friends. The words live in their own way – they travel, they find the people that need them. If you feel the world needs more positivity, more daring, fewer limits and more imagination, be the messenger, put it out there. You literally never know whose life you can change, whose compass arrow you can send spinning in an uncharted, inspired direction.

ANDY KNOWLTON Drunken Poet's Project *Found materials*

The Drunken Poet dolls are small dolls that I make by hand from trash I find on the streets. Each doll holds a little bottle and inside of the bottle, I put an original poem. I leave the dolls on the streets for people to find and keep. It feels like I am making a personal gift for someone, and hopefully, when they find it, they feel something special. I want to take people's minds off of their daily routines by surprising them with something unique. I have made over 200 dolls, and I leave them in different neighborhoods all over Seoul.

Breaking the Line

Harriet Fraser

Ingredients:
- England's deepest lake
- England's highest mountain
- England's favourite view
- A single oak tree
- A poem printed onto a line of yellow cloth

Place the yellow cloth on the fell, linking the tree and the lake.
Leave for one week.

*

Poetry that makes a statement or invites contemplation about environmental issues has many merits – in a concise way it can evoke so much more than lengthy prose. But its readership is often confined to the relatively small circles of those who like poetry or seek out environmental writing. So how might its impact be felt beyond such circles? There are more people out there who care about their

[opposite] ROB FRASER Wastwater and the line *Wasdale, Cumbria*
Although only 1.5 metres wide, the yellow line made a huge impact on the 4 km wall of scree and drew attention to a single oak tree that is seldom noticed.

Putting the line in place
Pegging the yellow twill in place with help from six volunteers on the wind-buffeted 30-degree slope, using 440 pegs with precision cutting around saplings along the way.

environment, right? People who might not read poetry but have an opinion and have plenty to say. So how might poetry get them talking?

One way might be to place a poem not on paper, but in the landscape, incorporating it into a visual art piece. This has become a central strand of my practice as a writer, and my collaboration work with my partner, photographer Rob Fraser, as we explore issues of environment and culture. With this poem I wanted to celebrate one particular oak tree, to mark the connection between this tree, the water that feeds it, and the sky above, and at the same time to prompt consideration of the actions of humans on the planet and the choices that face us as we grapple with the reality of our impact and a changing climate. I have done temporary installations several times, but this was different: I didn't go small, nor was the installation tucked away.

The oak tree stands on a steep scree slope above the shore of Wastwater in Wasdale, one of the Lake District's most dramatic landscapes. In fact, the view over the lake to the screes has won the accolade of 'Britain's favourite view'. Wasdale boasts raw and powerful scenes, with England's highest fells, the dark waters of its deepest lake, and awe-inspiring scree slopes that run almost vertically along one side of the lake and remain virtually inaccessible. The view has been unchanged in living memory.

I had the poem printed onto a 110-metre strip of cloth and headed into Wasdale in early May with a team of friends and strangers who wanted to get involved. We laid the cloth, pegged down carefully at 50cm intervals, from the trunk of the tree to the shores of the lake. The gap in the line – a practical necessity accommodating a path – became a symbol of human impact on the planet.

Everything is Connected

skyline
treeline
waterline
bloodlines
time circled inside this oak
future in the smooth trust of acorns

land falling into lake
earth into water
water into earth
nature's threads
certain and tenuous as breath

we are woven in
a part and yet apart

not knowing what may happen
when we break the line

Rob and I wanted the installation to provoke curiosity and conversations but didn't anticipate what would happen. Within one day comments on Facebook had reached their hundreds, the BBC had become involved and a debate had kicked off. Some people hated it, some people loved it. And people were asking: What is and isn't 'natural' about our landscapes? Can we really ignore what we are doing to the planet and the responsibility we share in the care of the world we live in?

Online and in the local area the debate continued. Some people were extremely angry that the view they loved had changed – even though the majority of these people wrote from far flung parts of the UK. Some threads included personal abuse. We were called 'idiots' and 'sick morons' (this last by someone whose profile shows he is a retired medical doctor) and we received threats including demands that we should be prosecuted or, worse, be strung up by the cloth and hanged, or have it forcibly stuffed up our backsides.

These kinds of comments were met with equally passionate calls for the installation to be celebrated because of the questions it provoked. Rob and I watched as comment after comment was posted and some very important issues were raised. What is natural? What is a wilderness? Do we notice individual trees? What is a perfect view? Whose view is it anyway, and should it always stay the same? What choices do we make about our individual and collective impact on the environment?

Here's an example from a Facebook thread (I have collected over 200,000 words worth of debate so far):

A: I can only hope that this ugly scar on one of the most unspoilt beautiful places in England is removed, without any traces, at the earliest opportunity.

B: Unspoilt. Totally. Apart from the pylons, cables, road, stone walls, buildings, acres of monoculture caused by grazing sheep, dams, constructed footpaths, buildings, pub, car park, constructed watercourses, signs, pine plantation, farms, farm machinery, portaloos and reservoir. How dare they put a piece of yellow ribbon in there for two weeks. The cheek of it, in OUR unspoilt valley!

C: I think what is interesting about the negative response is how people feel so much ownership over a natural landscape that they are so greatly offended when something intervenes with it and their idealised perception of what it 'should' be like.

Questions were raised about attitudes to pollution, to deforestation, to reforestation, to traffic, to nuclear power, to farming, to tourism. The installation also spurred a debate about the value of poetry and art to provoke questions, and it revealed a polarisation of thinking about art in Cumbria – for some people the 'natural beauty' of the countryside in England's largest and most celebrated national park is enough and art should be confined to museums; for others art in the landscape should be encouraged. For me, placing poetry in the landscape in unusual ways and using it to spark curiosity and conversations is exciting.

The National Park is a place that's designated for the enjoyment of 'everyone', but meeting this requirement is a very, very difficult thing to do. It is a place where biodiversity as well as a rich human culture, which includes activities from farming to fell running and art, as well as mass tourism, are all supported. The Lake District is not alone in having to deal with conflicting demands and the impossibility of pleasing people with opposing views, and the debate that is centred on a local event could be relevant to many other parts of the planet. The day that I wrote the poem for the line was the day that scientists declared that the deaths of numerous whales washed up on northern European beaches was caused by their consumption of plastic – just one of many events that demonstrate that, through human action, a line has been crossed, and something has been broken. The resonance of the poem written for a particular tree, in a very particular place, has, it seems, gone beyond its small surface area of 165 square metres.

What kind of view are we all attached to? Is it enough to continue to celebrate and promote a sublime, picturesque, chocolate-box image of our surroundings? What human impact on the land do we choose to turn a blind eye to? We offered the line and the poem as a reflection of nature's interconnections, with a suggestion that it is humans, rather than other aspects of the natural world, that most frequently disturb these connections, often with disastrous consequences. The idea of visualising the age of the earth as just 24 hours is well known, showing humans on this planet for what amounts to little more than a few minutes and with the enormous evolution of industry and pollution occurring in just a few seconds of that time. This single slim line set against a vast backdrop of earth and rock offered an alternative way to illustrate this.

This installation was part of a larger project, *The Long View*, which takes as its focus seven trees that Rob and I have chosen with great care over the past five years. The Wasdale Oak is the westernmost of the seven trees. While we are looking really closely at each tree and its surroundings, this was never going to be the only thing we did. You can't point to a single tree without quickly noticing that everything is connected. These last three words gave the installation its proper title, 'Everything is Connected' (although it was quickly given the name 'The Yellow Line' by others), and underpin much of our thinking. It's a view that's nicely summed up by Neil Postman, writing about the idea of Spaceship Earth in *The End of Education* (1996):

'We have here, then, a narrative of extraordinary potential: the story of human beings as stewards of the Earth, caretakers of a vulnerable space capsule. [...] If any part of the spaceship is poisoned, then all suffer – which is to say that the extinction of the rainforest is not a Brazilian problem; the pollution of the oceans is not a Miami problem; the depletion of the ozone layer is not an Australian problem [...] "Never send to know for whom the bell tolls," wrote

John Donne. "It tolls for thee." If ever there was a narrative to animate that idea, the Earth as our one and only space-ship is it [...] This is an idea whose time has come. It is a story of interdependence and global cooperation, of what is at the core of humanness; a story that depicts waste and indifference as evil, that requires a vision of the future and a commitment to the present.'

The plan was to leave the yellow line in place for up to two weeks, perhaps less if the weather forced us to take it away (it would be too heavy to remove after rain). When we received threats from unknown people who wanted to go in and remove it themselves, we knew we had to take it out early. It's not a simple task and although the keyboard warriors were most probably typing out empty threats, we couldn't be sure. Anyone going in unprepared would risk injury to themselves and to the environment. It was a physically demanding task, with 440 pegs to remove and cloth weighing almost 50 kilos to be rolled and unstitched, with care to work around tree saplings, and then carried out over unstable ground, on foot, a journey that takes ninety minutes. So we headed in as the sun was setting, with friends and with people we didn't know who had contacted us and wanted to help.

I made some notes the next morning as I stood on the opposite side of the lake, looking at the ghost of the line on the screes:

'The air is entirely still. Screes, trees, grass reflected in a still lake, blue sky edged with picture-perfect fluffy clouds. When we reached the Wasdale Oak last night at about 8.30pm a lone cloud rested on Great Gable and turned, slowly, from grey to white to salmon pink. The wind dispersed and we took the cloth away with a gentleness and calmness, three sets of people working opposite one another, pulling out pegs and rolling the yellow. Behind the cloth wood sorrel had put out delicate flowers; bracken was unfurling. The saplings we had cut round were a rich green. No flora or fauna were harmed in the making of this brief ephemeral work. Nothing harmed except perhaps people's sense of rightness or righteousness. And as well as the growth of flowers and ferns along the line there has been a growth of friendships – new friends made among a group of people who are willing and eager to support statements like this and say, it's OK, just for a few days, to put something different in front of people's eyes and suggest, just maybe, that it's worth considering our own points of view and the possibility of change.'

Killochries (excerpt)   Jim Carruth

vi. Storyteller

The old man talks in code:
fables and parables

biblical and otherwise.
Tonight it's a dairy heifer

who wouldn't accept
her place in the byre

but roared a protest
from her stall,

kicked out
at the clusters,

flicked her tail
in the dairyman's face.

She'd give up her
milk to no-one.

He leaves it there, tells me
the ending is not yet written.

*

I've had it.
Old man, open your eyes,
look around you – can't you see
this is not a success?

Tell me who has a wasted life.
On what basis do you judge me
from the heights of this hill?

I am sick of your prayers.
What are you thanking God for:

this year's ruined barley,
your bank manager's letters,
your dying mother,
your poverty?

Silence in that byre:
the old man's brief glance to me
an hour-long sermon.

*

At night I'm at him again.

Is silence not always
the church's answer?
Secrecy, collusion, cover-up

turning its back
on the vulnerable and weak
time and time again.

I've said too much;
this was never about the church.

He answers at last:

Better tae hae belief in ane hersh god
than tae hae lost faith wi many.

*

Morning comes.
Hen house silent,
       limp bodies,
a feathered shroud.

Why kill so many, fox,
when you can carry
        only one?

*

After months here
the hill has worn away
my few words.

My voice has let me down,
my hands are not mine.

A clumsy struggle
with an alien pencil that lies uneasy
on the hard skin.

I snap it like a stick,
cast the diary in the bin.

*

We try to ready the farm.

Up and down
the ladders

all afternoon,
hammering down
loose slates
with six-inch nails,
tethering
corrugated sheets
with bale string.

At night, outside
whistle, crash and shatter.

Inside, I breathe in
creak and strain.

*

Morning picks its way through the debris —
slates, guttering, sheets, broken glass.

A couple of trees have fallen
in the small wood,
the lone pine has lost its tip.

I turn my back on the farm,
take my anger up the hill.

Alone on this unforgiving muir
I rage at the old shepherd,
curse his King James Bible,
kick out at his blind faith,
wrestle with his god

and fall.

*

St John 10:13

The hireling fleeth,
because he is an hireling,
and careth not for the sheep.

*

He tells me a week later
he'd followed me,

watched me break down
in the field of whins,

cry for hours
on the hill –
all that outpouring

that understanding
of wasted years.

Ahint yir een-glint
a sma hairt sair skint.

[chronosequence]

Doireann Ní Ghríofa

Here, where decades of diggers' tracks
fill with murky puddles, here,
your phone fails
to find a signal. A starling
flits past. Say *lost*.

Strata:
This land was
once an oak forest,
translated to farmland,
then swallowed by a profit
crop of un-baubled
Christmas trees.
Say *industrial saws*.

Say *fall* and a scrape scrawls itself
on your hand, red under black mud. The sky darkens.
Follow clawed paw-prints. Think wolf. At a crossroads,
choose left. Feel your socks grow wet.
Say *roof* and see it – there – a sudden peak
that tilts the gap between trees. Walk towards it fast,
hoping for a yard with a jeep, a sheepdog, a cup of tea.

Derelict.
The house is an abandoned relic. Uninhabited,
it draws you towards its unlocked door,
as though you could be an owner,
but know that you are a tourist
here, nothing more.   Say *silence*.
Under your fingertips, walls crumble. Say *rubble*
and stumble in. Stair-steps sag underfoot. Say *bed*
and you will see it, still pink-quilted, with a pillow
dotted with fallen plaster. On the sill, a bible lies
open, pages sun-bleached, words evaporated.

                                        Strata:
                                    In layers
                                of wallpaper,
                            in repeated splits
                        of tears from tears,
                        cleaved from old
                            paint below,
                        a broken skin
                            exposed
                    to reveal bone-
                    white plaster
                underneath. Feel
                    this dwelling
                shred itself back

                                        to brick, back
                                          to cracked
                                       cement, back
                                         to ground
                                             where,
                                        deep under
                                        wild grass,
                                       roots of oak
                                       are held still
                                            in dirt.

Say *parlour*. There, a chair aims away
from the cracked glass of an ancient TV
and turns towards the window instead.
In wind, a ragged net curtain blows in. Sit.
Sit and imagine yourself become someone
else. Watch the window as they once did.
Birdsong. Nettles and brambles sway. A crab-apple
blossom is drawn through the gap, lifted in
to land in your lap. A gift. Another word
comes to you then, unsummoned: *bláth*.

                                            Strata:
                                      Who could sing,
                                          still, here?
                                      Say *starling*,
                                      bird who fills

air with inherited
sound, speckled
imitations, recalled,
passed down. A bird's
remembered soundscape.
From a stranger's chair,
you listen and translate its song:

sheep's bleat, click of wireless, beer-bottle hiss,
boots clickclack on cobbles, child's giggle,
weep-gulps, stream babble, chicken
-claw scritch-scratch, strike of a match

Say *starling* – starling
who listens, who lifts
shreds of us away,
who records and remembers
sounds we once made. See
this little mimic who will sing
of us to his sons and daughters.
Say *inheritance*.

Word Soul

Daniel Nakanishi-Chalwin

On early Japanese poetry,
its magical origins and techniques

Take a walk around a word. I have always found 'dungeon' to be particularly accommodating. The dread finality of that first syllable echoing, via the consonance of /n/, through the moist, oozing space of the second. I cannot, of course, discount my knowledge of the meaning of the word in helping to conjure this chthonic image, but the sounds alone still do something strange to my head, still make a place I can explore.

Is 'dungeon' complete, self-enacting – a one-word poem? I am not sure. But I think I know what poetry isn't. It isn't the preferred medium of our current 'civilisation', glutted as it is with data, frantically distracting itself as the biosphere screams. It isn't that language that has been commodified along with everything else, the vacant cant of marketing and politics (itself a kind of marketing). It certainly isn't 'dungeon's' newspeak cousin, 'extraordinary rendition', or the soothing cadences of 'quantitative easing' – phrases both with immaculate surfaces, as unrevealing of inner depth as Botoxed faces. Whilst every single word of a poem need not be as evocative as 'dungeon', we expect combinations of them, their interacting tensions, to build a heightened language, to sing. It is unsurprising to discover that the traditional term for poetry in Japan, *uta*, has the double meaning of 'song'. As in all cultures, the voice is the source.

Poetry thus begins as elevated, sung, literally en-*chanted* speech. This is the 'word-hoard' of the Anglo-Saxons, precious and special. This is the *kotodama* or 'word soul' of the ancient Japanese. One of the earliest references to kotodama in the written record comes from a poem by Yamanoue no Okura (AD 660–c.733), which appears in the *Man'yōshū*, the *Collection of Ten Thousand Leaves*, the oldest existing anthology of Japanese verse.

Kamuyo yori	From the Age of Gods
Iitsutekuraku	This has been the saying passed down:
Sora mitsu	Sky-seen Yamato
Yamato no kuni wa	Is a land hallowed in power
Sumekami no	Wielded in the hand
Itsukushiki kuni	Of a sovereign deity,
Kotodama no	A land where the word soul
Sakiwau kuni to ...	Works its potency for weal ...[1]

Japanese prosody is based on alternating lines of five and seven syllables, the haiku being the form most familiar in the West (three lines of 5–7–5). The poem above follows this rule, but is of a much older style, where the ultimate length was at the discretion of the poet. Written on the occasion of the dispatch of a diplomatic mission to T'ang China, it runs on for an additional 55 lines. This is expansive public verse, high rhetoric to enhance the status of the Japanese court at Yamato, to bolster a tiny nation against its huge continental neighbour. It is also a benediction, a spell, as its title makes plain – 'A poem for a good departure and a good return.'

Koto- ('word') dama ('soul') was the power of language to affect reality by appealing to the gods. Although now written with the character for 'word' or 'speech' (言), *koto* is a homonym with a separate meaning of 'matter, affair, incident' (written with a different glyph, 事). In ancient times, however, it appears little or no distinction was made between the two.[2] Words were synonymous with reality, a self-fulfilling wish. To call Yamato a hallowed land was to make it so; to compose the lines 'Go without mishap, / Safe in the power of your luck, / And quickly return, my lord' was to weave a protective veil over one of its representatives at the start of a hazardous journey overseas. In a similar vein are the *Man'yōshū*'s numerous 'land-viewing' poems, written as part of a ritual describing and praising the imperial realm. Felicitous turns of phrase pleased the many gods that dwelled there, energising the earth itself to prevent natural disasters and ensure bountiful crops (not to mention political stability).

Vivid evocations of landscape are in fact a hallmark of the anthology as a whole, not the exclusive preserve of overt public ceremonial. Poems by named princes and aristocrats sit alongside anonymous 'folk' verse. There are private love poems and formal elegies, verse about hunting, travelling and the hardships of poverty. In some cases, the refined elegance of Chinese literature is a strong influence, but the overriding aesthetic is of a vigorous native beauty. Mist and the moon, fragrant pine trees and glittering seaweed, the crumpled-up mountains of a richly volcanic land, the crashing surf of its rocky shores. It is a vibrant world built partly through *makurakotoba* or 'pillow words', fixed formulas that adorn certain place names or natural phenomena: 'the madder-red sun', 'sweet-wine Miwa Mountain', 'Nara of the blue-green earth', 'Fujie of the rough-bark cloth'.[3]

These makurakotoba are reminiscent of epithets in Homer, where Odysseus is repeatedly described as 'many-wiled' (*polumetis Odysseus*) and the dawn as 'rosy-fingered' (*rhododactylos eos*).[4] For Homer, they served as metrical ballast to fill out the line and, through their repetition, also aided the memorisation of (extremely) long oral poems. The purpose of pillow words is somewhat different. To understand what they do, it is necessary to return to the gods and the primacy of the voice.

Landscape panegyrics and poems for safe journeys were required because of the capricious nature of Shintō deities. In this animist religion, everything shimmers with a numinous otherness, from trees and plants to rocks and the ocean. Everything is in flux and in need of diligent ritual to keep it mollified and benign. Divining the will of the myriad gods was therefore vital and was achieved in the late prehistoric age through the *miko*, a female shaman or oracle. The *Nihonshoki* (*Chronicles of Japan*), compiled like the *Man'yōshū* in the eighth century AD, records a rite in which Empress Jingū herself acted as miko. To the accompaniment of a *koto*, or zither, played in order to coax a deity into manifesting itself, the Empress became, through trance, the voice of a god:

> *Kamukaze no Ise no kuni no, momozutau Watarai no*
> *agata no, sakusuzu Isuzu no miya ni masu kami, na wa*
> *Tsukisakaki-Itsuno-Mitama-Amazakaru-Mukatsuhime-*
> *no-Mikoto nari.*

> I am the god in the shrine of split-bell Isuzu in the district
> of hundred-transmit Watarai in the province of divine-
> wind Ise, and my name is Tsukisakaki-Itsuno-Mitama-
> Amazakaru-Mukatsuhime-no-Mikoto.[5]

It is worth noting that a pillow in ancient Japan was not a soft, downy object. A bundle of grass at its most improvised, it was usually a wooden block, a simple pedestal to raise the head. In this god's grand self-introduction, 'split-bell' (*sakusuzu*), 'hundred-transmit' (*momozutau*) and 'divine-wind' (*kamukaze no*) are all pillow words, *elevating* the proper nouns they modify, marking them out as extraordinary, sacred places. Even the name of the deity has a makurakotoba embedded in it – *amazakaru*, meaning something like 'distant skies'. Furthermore, the rhythm of the speech itself approximates very roughly the repeating pattern of five and seven syllables so basic to classical verse (it begins 5–6–5–9–4 ...). It seems Japanese poetry may have grown from the specialised language of shamanic ritual just as much as from song.[6] The koto (or zither) appears to confirm this link; poetry too was often performed to its music. Enchanted language, indeed.

The magical aura surrounding pillow words is intensified by the fact that their meaning is often obscure or non-rational. Some are true epithets, conveying an essential quality of the word they crown. Ise is of the 'divine wind' because it was (and still is) the site of a major shrine. As the source of a certain pigment, Nara naturally becomes 'of the blue-green earth'. But Fujie ('of the rough-bark cloth') was not a centre for textile production. It acquires its makura-kotoba purely through wordplay – *fuji* (藤), the first ideograph of its name, means 'wisteria', a raw material for making cloth. The import of other pillow words has been lost completely over time; they remain cryptic despite several hundred years of scholarship. When translating poems from the classical into the modern language, Japanese academics often therefore leave the pillow words in parentheses, aloof from the body of the poem, unconnected to its semantic content. For Watanabe Yasuaki, this is because their chief power is as sound and rhythm. They act like triggers or spells – *abracadabra!* – calling up the word that follows and charging it with significance.[7]

Azusayumi	Taut catalpa bows
Haruyama chikaku	Spring mountains close at hand
Ie oreba	You've built your house,
Tsugite kikuramu	And you must live with cries of warblers
Uguisu no koe	Continually about your ears.

– Anonymous
(p.668)

Like the koto in Empress Jingū's trance ritual, the catalpa bow was a shamanic tool, an instrument plucked to invoke a deity. Here it is the pillow word that calls forth 'spring (*haru*) mountains (*yama*)' through *haru*, a homonym also meaning 'to stretch / make taut' (as in a strung bow). The first two lines thus literally mean 'catalpa bow / **stretch-spring** mountains nearby'. Whereas 'Fujie' leads to 'bark cloth' through the logical intermediary of 'wisteria', here the connection is a mere coincidence of sound. A pun.

The pun does not enjoy an exalted reputation in the West. Most often it represents puerile humour. ('Did you hear about the constipated mathematician? He worked it out with a pencil.') In poetry its closest equivalent is probably the limerick, with its serendipitous rhymes. ('There was a young lady from Leeds / Who swallowed a packet of seeds,' which had a deleterious effect on her digestion.) At a rather more sophisticated level there is, of course, Shakespeare. His verse drama teems with mercurial punsters, artful quibbling being language his audiences obviously enjoyed, although no one could accuse Lady Macbeth of being some kind of proto-stand-up.

> If he doe bleed,
> Ile guild the Faces of the Groomes withall,
> For it must seeme their Guilt.[8]

Utterly ruthless, she will frame the poor grooms, smearing them with the golden, kingly blood of the murdered Duncan. She will 'gild' them with 'guilt'. A pun, yes, but hardly rib-tickling.

Japanese, with its abundance of homonyms (we've already seen koto as 'word', 'affair' and 'zither'), is even riper territory for word-play than English. And while punning is a respectable mainstay of its comedy, along with slapstick and mugging (funny faces, not robbery), in poetry it becomes what the Shakespearean scholar Kenneth Muir called the 'uncomic pun'.

Katakai no	In Katakai
Kawa no se kiyoku	River the shallows are clear,
Yuku mizu no	The water flows
Tayuru koto naku	Never ceasing I shall come
Arigayoimimu	Again and yet again to gaze.

– Ōtomo no Yakamochi
(AD 718?–785)
(p.620)

The fourth line (*tayuru koto naku* / 'never ceasing') is a *kakekotoba* or 'pivot word', referring simultaneously back to the flowing river and forward to the visiting poet. It pings the sense of the poem in both directions, enacting the very ceaseless movement it describes. It is also a doubling that places individual feeling within the wider, divine landscape.

Kono yama no	Close above the peak
Mine ni chikashi to	Of this mountain range I saw
A ga mitsuru	The rising moon –
Tsuki no sora naru	Whose track is far across a sky
Koi mo suru kamo	No more empty than my love.

– Anonymous
(p.690)

In the poem about Katakai River, the pivot word has twin frames of reference (river / gazing poet), but one uniform meaning throughout ('never ceasing'). In this verse about the moon, both frame and meaning are doubled. *Sora*, the pivot word in the fourth line, is homonymous ('sky' and 'distracted / restless'); it becomes 'the sky with the moon in it' in the phrase '*tsuki no sora*', and, at exactly the same time, 'my excited, restless love' in the succeeding, and overlapping, phrase, '*sora naru / Koi*'. Difficult to render precisely in English, the translator has wisely opted for a comparative structure instead, which conveys the correspondence between natural object and human emotion, but which loses the peculiar impact of the original Japanese. As with the bowstring-spring-nexus earlier, 'moon sky' seems to summon up 'restless love', but the effect is bigger, permeating the entire sense of the poem. Watanabe Yasuaki has described it as like hearing a voice in stereo (true even when the poem is read silently in one's head).[9] Personally, I prefer the analogy of double tracking, the recording technique favoured by John Lennon for the vocals in his solo work. There is an uncanny thickening of sound, a layering, the weirdness of two-in-one. We return to the image of the shaman in her trance, channelling the words of a god. The voice is simultaneously hers, and yet not hers. The voice is a vehicle, a matryoshka doll, a vessel containing something else. Even a private verse about feverish love acquires the heightened atmosphere of a religious ritual.

With their extremely dense use of language, both pillows and pivots expand a poem beyond the constraints of form. Unlike Yamanoue no Okura's 63-line epic or even the prolix declarations of the deity from divine-wind Ise, over 90% of poems collected in the *Man'yōshū* are *tanka* ('short poems') of five lines and 31 syllables (5–7–5–7–7). Within this small space, words demonstrate their own irrepressible life force. Trading meanings amongst themselves, they become as slippery, as animate, as the world of rivers, mountains and warblers that they evoke. A comment by Kenneth Muir about the Shakespearean uncomic pun is particularly apt – '[Puns] seem to shoot out roots in all directions, so that the poetry is firmly based on reality – a reality which is nothing less, if nothing more, than the sum total of experience.'[10]

All of which makes Japan the Land of the Rhizome Pun, where even the words, like young bamboo, are good eating. The most obvious modern incarnation of kotodama, that old belief in the soul of words and their equivalence with the things they denote, is the tradition of *o-sechi* or New Year's food. All of the elaborate dishes are highly symbolic, designed to bring about good fortune through a menu of spell-like puns. *Kuro-mame* are 'black beans', signifying one's ability to 'work hard' (an additional meaning of *mame*), labouring until one is deeply tanned or 'black' (*kuro*). To eat herring roe (*kazu no ko*) is to request the continued prosperity of one's family line, for its name literally means 'many children'. Other edible quibbles represent longevity, wealth, academic success or bumper harvests. Magic – which once left the mouth of the entranced shaman or praise-smith poet as sound – now re-enters it as food.

What is poetry? The shape-shifting vitality of language makes it hard to answer that question, to pin the creature down in straightforward, rational terms. In the case of early Japan, poetry constructs a resonant space that forever exceeds its own dimensions, a world that grows to be identical with the 'real' world that surrounded and sustained its creators. Through a sort of feedback loop, the human voice is transformed into the voice of the deified universe itself. Any talk of the poetic also automatically implies its opposite, the prosaic, and reminds us that abuses of language are not without their cost. 'Extraordinary rendition' sticks in the craw like a string of lab-made polymers. There is no nourishment here. I, for one, would much rather sit down to a hearty slice of 'dungeon'.

Notes

1. Translation by Cranston, E. A. *A Waka Anthology – Volume One: The Gem-Glistening Cup*, Stanford University Press, 1993, pp.364–366. All subsequent translations of poems by Cranston. Page refs. given after each poem.
2. Sasaki, T. *Kotodama to wa Nani ka [What is Word Soul?]*, Chūōkōron-Shinsha, 2013, p.4.
3. All translations by Cranston, *op. cit.*, p.210, p.176, p.377, p.199 respectively.
4. Fenton, J. *An Introduction to English Poetry*, Penguin, 2003, pp.40–41.
5. My translation, based closely on that by Aston, W. G. *Nihongi: Chronicles of Japan from the Earliest Times to AD 697*, Charles E. Tuttle, 1972, p.225.
6. For this theory see Blacker, C. *The Catalpa Bow – A Study of Shamanistic Practices in Japan*, Japan Library, 1999, p.112. The author is herself channelling the ideas of Nakayama Tarō.
7. Watanabe, Y. *Waka to wa Nani ka [What is Japanese Poetry?]*, Iwanami Shoten, 2009, pp.36–37.
8. Spelling as given in Muir, K. 'The Uncomic Pun' in *Cambridge Journal Vol.3*, May 1950, p.474.
9. Watanabe, *op. cit.*, p.56.
10. Muir, *op. cit.*, p.483.

On seeing Iran in the news,
I want to say

Marjorie Lotfi Gill

my grandmother was called Nasrin,
that she died two years ago in Tabriz
and I couldn't go to say goodbye,
that she knew nothing of power,
nuclear or otherwise. I want to say
that the fires for *Chahar Shanbeh Suri*
were built by the hands of our neighbours,
and as children we were taught to jump
and not be caught by the flame. I want to say
my cousin Elnaz, the one born after I left,
has a son and two degrees in Chemistry,
and trouble getting a job. I want to say
that the night we swam towards
the moon hanging over the horizon
of Caspian Sea, we found ourselves
kneeling on a sandbar we couldn't see,
like a last gift. I want to say
I'm the wrong person to ask.

Scientist as Poet as Scientist   Jeff Ollerton

For as long as I can recall I have been a scientist. Early memories as a child include turning over rocks and probing under bushes in search of elusive insects, dissecting knowledge from road kill, and splitting it from fossil-rich shale. But also, for as many years as I can remember, I have created poetry. Sometimes this has been permanent written text, other times only thoughts and fragments, committed to temporary memory and ultimately lost like the bugs I studied in jars and released back into the wild. Over time the science has become public-facing as hobbies were turned into a career. The poetry remained turned inward, written for myself, only occasionally on show to lovers or to audiences at local spoken-word events.

Perhaps the idea of scientist as poet is too contradictory to bear serious scrutiny, but both of these aspects of my life relate to a deep, enquiring curiosity that has always been present. Both reflect a need to understand something of this complex, confusing world we inhabit, and the place of people and their relationships with one another, and with the environment in a wider, encompassing nature.

In the first volume of *Dark Mountain* I stepped out as a scientist-poet and contributed an essay-with-poetry entitled 'W(h)ither Science?', which was a very personal take on the role of scientists, and the knowledge they generate, in the early 21st century. This piece was framed within the context of Uncivilised ideas of 'what happens when it all goes wrong?' I prefer to think of it as 'if' rather than 'when' because, as I originally put it, 'knowledge is not predictable'. In other words, we don't know what will happen in the future, so we can only prepare for a range of outcomes. If we take the best of the sciences and of the arts, and of the education they generate, perhaps we can survive as a species and as a set of communities.

Was that really only six years ago? So much has happened in the intervening period; the science has turned ever more outward, with more writing for scientific journals, magazines, my blog, and more presentations of the research undertaken by my group to other scientists, to policy makers and NGOs, and to the public. The poetry, meanwhile, has remained private, which led me to consider whether it was time to give up a little more. The two short poems in this essay were both written more than ten years ago, though they have been revised and polished periodically. Even as I began to construct this piece I was revising words and reconsidering sentence structure, much as I might revise the analysis of a data set or reconsider its interpretation when writing a scientific paper. One of the things I love about producing poetry is that its form is malleable, it's never complete, I can change it when I wish. This malleability is also a feature of science: we revise our ideas when confronted with new evidence, rejecting previously supported hypotheses in favour of more accurate notions of the universe.

Chains of Copper, Locks of Lead

Mention a river:
I may have heard of it,
Or talked to a woman who has gazed at its bed.
Cage its waters, bind its banks,
With chains of copper, and locks of lead.

Ultimately bending to time, eroding
The surge and the volume sustaining, removing.

Weighed down, I lay down,
And the river unconscious
Passed over my body and on to the sea.
While my lover cast stones from the bank to the current.
The banks of my body, the river of me.

Due to their inherent chemical properties, both lead and copper are relatively ductile, weak metals: they cannot withstand the force of a river indefinitely. In the same way, no matter how much we believe we can tame rivers or seas or any other component of the natural world, ultimately the environment will prevail. It just takes time. We might canalise a river to prevent flooding or dam it to provide hydro-electricity, but not realise that in its untamed state the river is more valuable, as it provides food, allows travel, brings fertility to flood plains. What, then, does it mean to 'know' something about a river? Whose knowledge is more valuable, which expert do we trust? The internet is awash with information, but knowledge, first and second-hand, can both enlighten us and sometimes prevent us from really understanding.

Ordinary by Choice

She chose the route and chose her topics,
Modular waypoints across years of work.
Decisions based on the balance of a gyroscopic
Pursuit of life, work, and an honours degree.
Finally, she elected to be
Ordinary by choice.

A student who chooses not to complete a final year dissertation module – and so graduate with Honours – but rather exit university with an Ordinary degree, is described as 'Ordinary by choice'. The phrase strikes me as both poetic and prophetic. Could anyone choose to be 'ordinary', and even if they could, is such a thing desirable? Is the course of a simple, ordinary life preferable to one that is complex and extra-ordinary? Does anyone truly believe that their experience of our rich, intricate world, in which decisions are made about priorities and 'balance of life', is ordinary, no matter how they make a living or what they do to fill their days?

Education in its widest sense, both formal and informal, taught and autodidactic, is a constant and destinationless journey that takes us from ignorant to less-than-ignorant. It is no coincidence that we use the same word ('course') in education, and to describe a river, and a life. A river's function, as far as people are concerned, depends on choices that we make as to its course and fate. But even without human intervention that course naturally shifts over time and its destination is not necessarily the sea: much depends on geological events and the resulting topography of the land, at time scales uncaptured by the course of an individual's experience.

The scientific research that I undertake is an attempt to capture truths about the ecological functioning of our planet and how it underpins human societies, no matter how technological or industrialised. It takes collected, often hard-won, data, internally scrutinises it for meaning, and externalises the findings into tables, graphs and written texts, that may influence other scientists or emerge in government reports or policy documents. My poetry takes ideas, emotions, feelings, and projects that mix of internal and external worlds into forms that sometimes, but not always, make sense to me. Empirical truths and emotional truths are not the same thing, and in fact may be contradictory and counter-factual. But empirical rationalism and emotional construction can coexist, and often do within the minds and personalities of scientists. Most do not produce poetry, but every scientist I know is emotionally invested in their subject and openly describes their science in terms of delight, rage, obsession, elation and disappointment, every bit as intense as any poet.

Climate Scientist Speaks

Helen Moore

*The Sibyl, with frenzied mouth uttering things not to be laughed
at, unadorned and unperfumed, yet reaches to a thousand
years with her voice by aid of the god.*

– Heraclitus

Our integrated Earth system is a thing of beauty –
the work of algorithms and differential equations.
In the calm of the lab, I sit by a plasma screen observing
the kaleidoscopic patterns of sea ice concentrations.
Through the laws and logic focussing my mind,
I peer into the future.

Arachne, our super-computer, makes 600 trillion calculations
per second, weaves scenes of spiralling instability.
With a tap on my touchscreen, I look through distant eyes in
    the sky –
polar orbiters that monitor deep-water currents, surface
temperatures and melting rates of glaciers and ice sheets.
Data drops into my office like subterranean water
in a limestone cave, leaving ever more profound impressions.

Often I'm gazing thousands of years into the past,
analysing cryospheric systems, evidence from borings in ice caps –
those giant, glassy scrolls chronicling periods of global heating
and cooling. Unforeseen results appear like rays of sunlight
piercing the atrium of a temple; then my mind fledges hypotheses
that rise on thermal currents. I race to track them down,
start the next phase of rigorous assessment.

When the media publishes my findings, or I report with colleagues
to Congress, there's always the hope that this time
our work will make a difference. Mostly I feel as if I'm speaking
with addicts on the subject of their habit –
the harm it's doing them and others, the denial of this truth.
Back home, I well up as my kids play at being adults –
their make-believe shaped by the only world they know.

O, but my angels, the unravelling web …

Ecology

Robert Wrigley

Study the muddy house, the salmon
gritting it out through the glacial till;
study the heart, which should not be seen
but heard, study the tree that is the child

and the ink that makes the octopus invisible.
Epistemologies of silence and blindness,
the suffering of common stones, the soul
with its hardened, scaly, inevitable callous:

study them by coyote light, buffalo magnification.
And study the imperatives of rain and snow
at the whim and fancy of the wind.
Study the wind. We will never know

what it desires beyond the elsewhere it is going.
Study elsewhere, the geography of strange beds
and topography of lips and the glowing,
enormous, indefatigable possibilities of red.

The sky, which is the mother of all rivers,
must be studied, as must be the river of all mothers,
the oceans of spirit, the wells of unbelievers,
days like buckets full, arriving one after another

in the absence of an invisible engineer.
Study the balusters and balustrades, wall studs
of sedimentary stone, the skin, the downiest hair,
spring grass, the planetary grave, the blood-fed

soil of the body farm, the pentagramatic arm,
the cuticle and free margin parentheses enclosing
pink implications, the vast concupiscent charms
of the toes, the sleepy eye's slow closing.

In such time as you are given, study the house
within the house within the house you love in.
Know of it such portion as you are allowed,
and return to it to die, like the salmon.

After a Live Stranding

David Knowles

A family of 13 pilot whales came ashore at Ballyness,
Donegal, July 2014.

It was just that the whales were the first.
We can see that now, perched
on the last slim ledge of our future, looking down
at them with their long, long wave lengths catching the message
we refused to see in the tides.

That was before, when the unquiet mix of forebodings,
        visions, rumours
lay so heavy on the soft sand of the few hearts that still beat.
That was before.

Before the mass self-immolations at the gates of the refineries.
Before the synchronised stunts with butcher knives,
like samurai unloading their own abdomens back onto the counters
of the fast-food giants.
Before the Reformed Mothers' Guild outings for mother and child
dashing in sensible shoes onto the rocks below.
Before it became clear that the price could never be paid
for treading carelessly on the dreams of the moon.

It's just that the whales were there first,
sifting their old lore for signs to the coming age.
And look, they brought their calves.
God help us, they brought their calves.

The Language of Lament Margaret Miller

Vancouver, where I live, is situated in a rain forest, so in a typical summer we have moderate temperatures and some rain – and sometimes a lot of rain. In the summer of 2015, though, we experienced extreme heat with almost no rain for months. In our garden the moss and ferns shrivelled and died. The trees were stressed. Neighbours' lawns turned brown. In the park down the street the ponds dried up and the fish and turtles living in them died and the birds and animals who fed there also suffered. Over the course of the summer we also learned more about the impact of the warm temperatures on salmon and other creatures in our oceans and rivers. Talk on the news was of a 'blob' of warm water floating off the coast. We now know that in British Columbia, as in the rest of the world, 2015 was the hottest summer on record, and 2016 looks to be warmer still.

At the height of our driest of summers I read *Extinction Dialogs: How to Live with Death in Mind,*[1] in which Guy McPherson and Carolyn Baker share their insights into how we might walk along the road we now find ourselves on. McPherson has studied the scientific data around climate change and the data tells him that not only is 'abrupt climate change' fully underway but that it is deadlier than asteroids. He takes the position that we have passed the point of no return; hope for an outcome other than mass extinction is delusion, or what he calls 'hopium'. Baker concurs with McPherson that the nations of the world are likely no longer able to 'do something'. For Baker, 'doing something' implies that the nations and the fossil fuel industry will come together and take the monumentally significant co-operative action needed to halt the death spiral we have entered. In her opinion the chances of this are nil.

196

McPherson and Baker know that for the many people who have come to the same conclusion this awareness leaves a deep sorrow for the earth and a profound need to grieve for our world. Baker observes that 'all of humanity has colluded in some manner with this ecocide, and we carry within us tremendous grief, guilt, emptiness, and fear.'[2] The world we are now inhabiting is akin to a hospice, and it is critical that we learn to grieve. Quoting psychotherapist Francis Weller:

> If we refuse or neglect the responsibility for drinking the tears of the world, her losses and deaths cease to be registered by the ones meant to be the receptors of that information. It is our job to feel the losses and mourn them. It is our job to openly grieve for the loss of wetlands, the destruction of forest systems, the decay of whale populations, the erosion of soil, and on and on. We know the litany of loss, but we have collectively neglected our emotional response to this emptying of our world. We need to see and participate in grief rituals in every part of this country.[3]

As part of her work Baker facilitates rituals to help people deal with their pain.

The tradition of lament poetry can be a valuable part of this process. Lament is a deep, ancient and universal form of human expression that has been created in diverse cultures and faith traditions. The Hebrew Bible, the tradition I am most familiar with, contains a treasury of lament poetry – these passionate expressions of grief and despair are found in the psalms, the Book of Lamentations and elsewhere. Biblical laments include individual and communal pleas to God for relief from illness or human-created disasters. In lament poetry the speaker may ask questions but receive no answers; there may be no hope. God may remain silent. In the Book of

Lamentations in particular there is a deeply felt absence of God. The lament was also the poetry of the prophets. As biblical scholar Walter Brueggemann observes, the great prophets were possessed of the poetic imagination to challenge the dominant reality; their poetry of lament had the power to cut through the illusion and denial that pervaded their society and viscerally announce that the state of the world was not right.[4]

We see in the work of these biblical poets, and in particular the counter-cultural vision of the prophets, laments for the suffering earth. Because of human actions, such as the scorched-earth warfare indulged in by foreign invaders and the appropriation of peasants' lands by the elites, the earth suffers and mourns.

> How long will the land mourn
> And the grass of every field wither?
> For the wickedness of those who dwell in it
> > the beasts and the birds are swept away,
> > because men said, 'He will not see our latter end.'
>
> > > (Jer 12:4)

> The earth mourns and withers,
> > the world languishes and withers;
> > the heavens languish together with the earth.
> The earth lies polluted under its inhabitants;
> for they have transgressed the laws,
> > violated the statutes,
> > broken the everlasting covenant.
>
> > > (Isa 24:4–5)

In the prophetic worldview, the land suffers because humans transgress against God and each other – the fate of the people and the land are intertwined. The prophets' poetic language pierces the people's denial and apathy, exposing and critiquing the social decisions that led to the land's destruction.

The lament tradition continues to be drawn upon by people around the world in a range of different social contexts. It has been adapted by the African-American community, by survivors of the Shoa, by victims of AIDS, by casualties of wars, and many others. Mining the deep cultural memory of their communities, the lament form gives these poets a means to express their suffering and grief.

The poetry of lament also creates a space where we are able to confront ourselves in the context of our broken relationship with the world. In his search for a contemplative approach to the environmental crisis, Douglas Christie finds inspiration in the 4th century Egyptian desert fathers' practice of *penthos*, the 'gift of tears', a practice that opened them to the fragility of existence and to all that is lost or in need of repair in society, nature and the cosmos.[5] This practice of deep mourning 'required courage, a willingness to face one's own fragility as well as the fragility and brokenness of the world. It meant refusing the temptation to evade the reality of those bonds that connect all beings to each other, and embracing the fact that one exists in a shared world.'[6] Christie sees this as a potentially valuable practice in the current historical moment, when 'a silence, like the silence of those increasingly barren habitats, weighs heavily upon us.'[7] As poetry has the capacity to bring forth the gift of tears it is the urgent job of poets (and other writers) to plumb our diverse cultural resources for the language that can embrace this reality, and so reveal the magnificence of the world that is being lost. Lament poetry, as part of human expression for thousands of years, offers a model of this kind of language.

Christie invites poets to bear witness to their loss, to name and describe it, and to open themselves up to feeling the loss as their own – for poets and their readers to, in effect, become mourners – arguing that this may well be one of the most important spiritual practices we can engage in at this moment. Whether we are able to give adequate expression to the catastrophic loss we are now experiencing is an open question, but for Christie even the possibility of being morally honest in our relationship with the natural world is difficult to imagine if we do not at least try to give voice to these losses.

Two poems, both from West Coast Canadian writers, are examples of this kind of work:

Litany
Catherine Owen

For a fad in feathers
in eighteenth-century milliners' shops
              the Carolina parakeet

For feline-prowess
in a mouseless lighthouse
              the Stephen's Island wren

For Mr. Odell's crackshot
              the Jamaican yellow macaw

For Ketil Ketilsson's
left boot

                the last Great Auk

For the palate of emperors

                  the auroch

For the hunger of sailors

                the Stellar's sea cow

For the ravaging of forests,
the despoiling of beaches,
the tainting of waters

                the Rapa snail, the Israeli gerbil
                and the hare-lipped suckerfish

For the cultivation of machinery
in rock quarries

                a tiny wild pansy and other
                statistics of rootlessness

Dank Tureen (a dream about global warming)
Susan McCaslin

Swimming the Australian crawl in a dank tureen,
the sides' sleek stainless steel without traction or edge

Treading water, slowly treading in a heavy dark
your once cold stiff fingers pumping blood
in a luxuriousness that gathers to a lukewarm
rush now becoming spa-like disarming soup
where you are swimming with the glorious beasts
the polar bear whose whiteness is God and the
shimmering fishes who have been here before you
and can teach you a few things about swimming
and your mother and father and sisters and brothers
and the Christ-Sophia floating on her cross upholding others
and the Buddha with his empty begging bowl afloat
and the homeless exiles, and deadbeat strangers
and the corporate heads with their swirling logos
circling toward the miasmic centre of a vortex
and the goats and cows and dogs and wolves
lapping with you faithfully round and round the rim
their large panting tongues and solemn eyes —

and this goes on all day, all night, and on and all till

you all scald and drown or drowning wake together

This poetry is of a type that, as Christie describes it, creates a moral-spiritual space that allows readers to experience their kinship with all beings in a larger, inter-related world, while we 'struggle to come to terms with losses so deep and extensive we can barely acknowledge them, much less absorb them or act in response.'[8]

So where does this all leave us? It seems clear that even if we intellectually know about mass species extinction, warming oceans and climate change, and know that these changes are rapidly altering the lives of people around the world, the harrowing nature of the problem has left many of us susceptible to the complacency and numbness that accompanies despair. We desperately need to grieve and lament poetry can move us in that direction. And from the place of deeper humanity that comes with grieving our eyes and hearts can open more fully to what is going on in the world around us. Grieving can, in effect, help us pay fuller attention.

To what we pay attention will, of course, depend on where we are. For myself, it could mean paying closer attention to the turtles, fish and birds that live in and around my local pond; I plan to get to know them a little better this year. Right now, paying attention means watching the fire that, as I write this, is ravaging Northern Alberta, in the area where the tar sand operations are located. Rising world temperatures have led to drier soil and vegetation, more lightning strikes and longer fire seasons, and this ever-expanding fire has already destroyed over half a million hectares of boreal forest – black and white spruce, aspen, jack pine. It has killed hundreds and thousands of the animals, insects and birds that live there – white-tailed deer, bumblebees, great horned owls, jack rabbits, grey wolves, black widow spiders, porcupines, and on and on. Smoke from the fire is so extensive that it is being breathed in thousands of kilometres away. Now the fire is moving on to the north-east and the more than 88,000 people who were forced to flee Fort McMurray will soon be returning, and the tar sands operations, which closed down temporarily as a result of the fire, will start up again soon. And the earth mourns.

Notes

1. McPherson, G and Baker, C. *Extinction Dialogs: How To Live With Death In Mind*, Tayen Lane Publishing, 2015.
2. Ibid, p.118.
3. Ibid, p.129.
4. Brueggemann, W. *The Prophetic Imagination*, Fortress Press, 2001.
5. Christie, D. *The Blue Sapphire of the Mind. Notes for a Contemplative Ecology*, Oxford University Press, 2013.
6. Ibid, p.77.
7. Ibid, p.83–4.
8. Christie, D., 2013, p.101.

No More

Em Strang

After Frank O'Hara

No more nice big daffodils
poking trumpets at the field
bare brass in March wind
so yellow

No more *Have you seen!* or
Did you know! with a book of birds
and fingers pointing at self
saliva there

No more tentativeness or bellyache
about lack of sparrows
or elitism of sparrow-hawks
on owned land

No more hare in the garden
frolicking because it's dead
or will be soon maggoty
if the world

No more bogus hallelujahs
inside the pristine forest

underneath the concrete
mind

No more important monkey
tomorrow in prize-winning feathers
on the steel penis podium
with *Here we are!*

No more welcome songs
repositioned eagles

No more return
reconstitution
restitution into something
holier than thou
or meatier

No more
moreness

The Problem of Describing Trees

Robert Hass

The aspen glitters in the wind
And that delights us.

The leaf flutters, turning,
Because that motion in the heat of August
Protects its cells from drying out. Likewise the leaf
Of the cottonwood.

The gene pool threw up a wobbly stem
And the tree danced. No.
The tree capitalised.
No. There are limits to saying,
In language, what the tree did.

It is good sometimes for poetry to disenchant us.

Dance with me, dancer. Oh, I will.

Mountains, sky,
The aspen doing something in the wind.

Dawn finds everything

hushed and muted, brittle grass bleached sage-white by frost.
Sunrise gleams back to meet itself in the water.
The day thaws and stretches:
gold leaves blaze against black trunks like long strips
punched out into darkness,
and then the lustre of the damp tarmac,
and stripes of low winter light spooling out through the trees,
and the cold, and rain shining on the bus windscreen:
a hundred thousand points of radiance,
quiet and exultant and unnoticed.

And elsewhere (or maybe closer in)
all the unspeakable things that people do to each other
– our vast capacity to justify, normalise, absorb –
and the wide truth, lying somewhere in all of this and
        everything else,
in holding all the beauty and all the atrocity and hurt,
in holding everything, loosely, spooling out like light,
like a great strip torn through the heart:
one long uncontrollable ceaseless rush
of everything that comes.

No More Words for Snow

Nancy Campbell

And if the sun had not erased the tracks upon the ice, they
would tell us of [...] polar bears and the man who had the
luck to catch bears.
– Obituary for Simon Simonsen, called
'Simon Bear Hunter' of Upernavik[1]

'Ilissiverupunga,' Grethe muttered. I'd only recently learnt the word.
It meant *'Damn! I've put it away in a safe place and now I can't find it.'*
Mornings at Upernavik Museum: an endless round of *kaffe* and
conversation as local hunters dropped by to discuss ice conditions.
Wishing to make progress in my research into Greenlandic literature,
I'd asked Grethe, the museum director, whether she knew of any
poetry books. But the bibliographic collections held mainly old
photographic records of the settlements, and kayaking manuals.

'Illilli!' Grethe called an hour or so later, *'There you are!'* She
emerged from a doorway almost obscured behind a stack of narwhal
tusks and proudly presented me with a 1974 hymnbook, its home-
made dust-wrapper culled from an offcut of pink wallpaper.

*

Upernavik is a small, rocky island on the west coast of Greenland.
At 72° north, it is well within the Arctic Circle, and the museum
claims to be the most northern in the world. The region's coastline is
described as 'an open-air museum'. That is to say, people suspect
there are interesting artefacts lying, undiscovered, everywhere under
the ice. No matter that they cannot be seen. They exist, and the empty

museum building awaits their arrival patiently. One of the museum's prize possessions is an old motorboat in which, during the short summer, Grethe visits people in distant coastal settlements who claim to have found an interesting specimen, perhaps a carved flinthead or an unidentified bone. As these visits are often combined with trips to distant family members and rarely seem to result in artefacts being brought back to the museum, the institution evidently fulfils a social function, knitting together isolated communities along the shores of Baffin Bay.

During my stay on Upernavik as writer-in-residence at the museum, I wanted to discover more about the contemporary poets of the Arctic. The local people I met denied any knowledge of such activity. Research doesn't always lead in the direction you expect: instead of books, it was my conversations with the islanders and observation of their interaction with the landscape that gave me a new perspective on the practice, and the endurance, of poetry in Greenland.

Grethe's hymnbook was a perfectly logical offering. In Arctic tradition, elevated verbal expression took the form of songs rather than poems. These songs have been roughly categorised as charms, hunting songs, songs of mood and songs of derision. The 'charms' were used in shamanic rituals to cast spells or cure illnesses, and were closely guarded secrets; they could be used, for example, to stop bleeding, make heavy things light, or call on spirit helpers. The other categories were public, being performed at feasts and flyting matches, accompanied by drumming and dancing. When the Danish explorer Knud Rasmussen began to transcribe the songs, he declared that his 'neat written language and [...] sober orthography [...] couldn't bestow sufficient form or force to the cries of joy or fear of these unlettered people'.[2]

The measure of 'poetic' success was that a song was *worth listening to*, as Tom Lowenstein demonstrates (in his translation of Rasmussen's transcription of a song by Piuvkaq):

I recognise what I want to put into words,

but it does not come well-arranged,

it does not become worth listening to.

Lowenstein describes the intense performance anxiety the poet might suffer: 'Forgetting the words, in a culture without paper, would be like losing the song. No-one would be there to prompt. It would be as if the words no longer existed at all.' This fear of forgetting is resonant, considering the losses faced by Inuit culture today, now that many traditional practices have fallen out of common use.

For a long time the Inuit 'did not know how to store their words in little black marks'.[3] They had no inclination to. Had they felt a need to apply their technical ingenuity to the problem of recording language, the course of bibliographic history might have been altered. As it is, publishing technology was introduced to Greenland by Danish missionaries during the late 19th century. The printing press preserved some legends, but the songs – because of their strong shamanic connections, not to mention occasional explicit content – were suppressed. The drums used in shamanic rituals were burnt in an attempt to oust 'heathen' beliefs, an act as sacrilegious as a book-burning in Europe.

Hushed and drumless, the Danish colonists tried to locate the rich sounds of *Kalaallisut,* the Greenlandic language, within their known orthography. The Roman alphabet was introduced to facilitate printing with conventional metal type imported from Europe. Kalaallisut, the standard dialect, is caught between cultures, one of the few Eskimo-Aleut languages to use an alphabetic rather than syllabic orthography (compare its close relative, Inuktitut or ᐃᓄᒃᑎᑐᑦ, found in Nunavut and the Northwest Territories, Canada). Yet what impact has two hundred years of printing made? In 2009 the *Unesco*

Kayaker in Ilulissat Icefjord, Greenland (photo: Nancy Campbell)

Atlas of the World's Languages in Danger designated Kalaallisut as being 'vulnerable' and predicted that the North and East Greenlandic dialects will disappear within a century.

*

When I began to learn Kalaallisut I had to ask my teachers to write the words down. They were bemused that I should find this more useful than hearing them spoken. Each time a word was written it would be spelt differently, and so the bemusement was passed on to me. Grethe told me that schools are not overly concerned about spelling: little children are bamboozled by the long words, and surely it is understandable that they get lost in the middle and miss out a few syllables? Teachers are more inclined to indulge the children than instil superficial spelling conventions.

Many of the islanders found expressing themselves in writing challenging. Speech is still the touchstone for communication: mobile phones and Skype are just as popular in Greenland as they are in the UK, whereas emails are approached with even more dread. It seems inevitable that future Arctic archives will be as sparsely furnished as those of the past.

I began to find English finicky and prim in contrast with Kalaallisut. As though they were knucklebones used in a game of dice, I shook up my tiny words and scattered them before my audience, having little influence on the score. Kalaallisut is more densely woven than English, with its smaller alphabet (18 letters) and polysynthetic words. When it is spoken, the suffixes are uttered so softly that an untrained ear cannot hear them. Sentences seem to trail off into silence.

Kalaallisut will use a single word to express a concept that English tiptoes around with a phrase. I was delighted to find signifiers for 'the sea rises and falls slowly at the foot of the iceberg' (*iimisaarpoq*) and 'the air is clear, so sounds can be heard from afar' (*imingnarpoq*). The language is famous for its many words for snow. This wide vocabulary for environmental conditions is of fundamental importance in understanding the Arctic ecology. As Barry Lopez points out in his book *Arctic Dreams*, contemporary scientists who arrive in the Arctic to assess climate change without a grasp of Kalaallisut risk being as crude as the early explorers who rushed to make their conquests of the North Pole without using established Inuit techniques for transportation and survival on the ice.

A map by the cartographer R.T. Gould in the National Maritime Museum in London delineates the last known steps of one such expedition led by Sir John Franklin, an ambitious Victorian quest to find the North-West Passage (1845–8). Gould's map depicts a land marked not by geographical features but by ominous 'x's: caches of letters, pemmican and bones found by search parties. These clues to Franklin's disappearance, linked by a red dotted line, eventually peter out in a question mark surrounded by blank paper.

The North-West Passage can be located by satellite these days, and few uncharted regions remain for those wishing to make their reputation as explorers. Yet despite advances in knowledge, Arctic geography still challenges the complacency of the modern traveller. Much of the visible environment is characterised by transience. The Pole is a shifting entity rather than a fixed point. Icebergs drift along the horizon, an ever-changing mountain range. The shore-fast ice forms an increasingly unpredictable border between land and sea; it disappears almost as fast as the tracks that pass across it. The geographer Nicole Gombay writes that these conditions 'require an awareness that the future cannot be predicted. As a result, people must focus on the present. Inuit have often told me, "Today is today, and tomorrow is tomorrow. Don't bring today into tomorrow, and don't bring tomorrow into today."'⁴ People's distrust of fixing future plans is balanced by 'an ability to let go of the past'. As Heraclitus might have said, it is impossible to step on the same ice floe twice.

*

Some mornings when I sat down to write at my desk overlooking the harbour, the sea outside my window seemed like a 'black cauldron covered with dark frost smoke' (as Robert Scott once described the phenomenon in his Antarctic journals). Other days, it was hidden by ice, and I watched the hunters make their way across the perilous expanse until they were just little black marks in the distance. The shadowy figures stepped carefully, pausing often, and tested the ice with their chisels before putting any weight on it. They were adept at interpreting patterns and sounds in the ice, which told them where to step to avoid falling into the freezing water. Each man's understanding of the ice was essential to his survival. (Once upon a time, the intense dangers faced during such expeditions had inspired the composition of songs, and even provided a metaphor for the process of composition: in a common trope, 'the right words' are as elusive to the singer as a seal or a caribou.)

The hunters' ramshackle workstations awaited their return. These *illukasik* had no walls, no roofs and no doors. There was nothing to obsure a hunter's view of his terrain, and nowhere to hide a secret. Domestic objects were left to rust under the open sky. The snow was a part of these skeletal structures as well as their backdrop; deep drifts were conscripted as tool racks. Ladders were lashed to the upright timbers but rather than providing a means of ascent they held struts together or secured them to the ground. Green twine wound about the cornices in endless orbits that stood in for more sturdy knots. The whole island appeared to be held together by an armature of twine and chicken wire beneath the snow.

Illukasik evolve. Beams are nailed to the joists, clothes racks tied to the beams. Sealskins are sewn to stretching frames and fish are hung up to dry out of reach of ravenous dogs. An accumulation of clothes pegs, knives and beer bottles adds a distinct signature to each hunter's creation. Between snowfalls, the outer boundaries of the illukasik are pitted with holes cast by phlegm, drops of oil and cigarette butts. Fresh lines of blood are traced across the island nightly as seal carcasses are hauled from the successful hunters' plots to waiting kitchens.

Sometimes, silhouetted in twilight, the illukasik looked like creatures rising from the sea. In these manmade objects I sensed something more than functional architecture. Folk tales describe hunters who created living monsters, *tupilak*, from sticks and stones and breath. The traditional Inuit religion is animist, and the culture is

A hunter's illukasik, high on the rocks overlooking Disko Bay, Greenland
(photo: Nancy Campbell)

strongly influenced by the belief that an *inue* or soul imbues every
material thing, from a rock to a harpoon head, informing its purpose.
And so, as the wind howled around the illukasik, I thought of them
as expressive marks on the landscape, almost akin to song. While
Inuit songs were intensely personal, and singing another's composition without crediting the original author was frowned upon, the
singers employed respectful variations on traditional themes. The
ikiaqtagaq or 'split song' was a conversation over time, its lyrics
added to, and developed, by successive singers. Likewise, the design
and materials of these improvised buildings diverged little from those
I had seen in old photographs in the museum. Here was the continu-
ation of a creative tradition that I sought.

When you store something away in a safe place, there's always the danger you won't find it again. Perhaps it is simpler to accept loss at the outset. The absence of printed language in the Arctic seemed to be as potent as the more tangible literature I had grown up with. I wondered whether a poet writing in English today could be active without publishing, and even whether there might not be a case for silence as a poetic stance in a culture so unremittingly orientated towards self-preservation and self-promotion?

With these thoughts I turned from the museum's bookcase (or, as I had learnt, *illisivit* – the root word of ilissiverupunga) to the gallery vitrines. There I found evidence left by earlier visitors: barometers and log books from explorers' vessels, and the highlight of the collection – the Kingittorsuaq Runestone, engraved with a short text by three Norsemen around 800 years ago and left in a cairn on a nearby island. Only the men's names could be read; the second half of their message is lost, written in mysterious characters that can't be deciphered, even by experts. The truncated story of these Viking travellers is emblematic of the history of the Norse in Greenland. None of these settlers would survive the 15th century, in part because they were unable to withstand the cooling climate of the Little Ice Age.

With the media saturated by images of the Arctic, it seems no longer necessary to convey its appearance, but rather the timbre of its many voices. The anthropologist Edmund Carpenter suggests that in cultures where transience is more evident, process is valued over preservation:

> Art and poetry are verbs, not nouns. Poems are improvised, not memorised; carvings are carved, not saved. The forms of art are familiar to all; examples need not be preserved.

When spring comes and igloos melt, old habitation sites are littered with waste, including beautifully designed tools and tiny carvings, not deliberately thrown away, but, with even greater indifference, just lost.[5]

It is increasingly apparent that our planet, including all its museums and libraries, is facing a devastation even more extreme than that of the great Alexandrian repository. Gombay addresses Western society as well as that of the Inuit, saying, 'In the face of knowledge that ultimately we are at the mercy of forces over which we have no control, how are we to react? We can choose to ignore such awareness – dig in our heels and do all that we can to find a means of establishing supremacy over the essential instability of existence, or, we can give in to it and accept that our experience is ephemeral.'[6] When the last of the ice has melted, the vanished tracks upon it will be the least of our concerns. No-one will be there to prompt. It will be as if words never existed.

Notes

1. Quoted in Hansen, K. *Nuussuarmiut: Hunting Families on the Big Headland*, Meddelelser om Grønland, vol. 345: Man & Society, vol. 35, 2008, p. 146.
2. Rasmussen, *Eskimo Folk Tales*, Kessinger Publishing, 2010.
3. *Ibid.*
4. Gombay, N. '"Today is today and tomorrow is tomorrow": Reflections on Inuit Understanding of Time and Place' in Collignon B. & Therrien M. (eds), *Orality in the 21st century: Inuit discourse and practices. Proceedings of the 15th Inuit Studies Conference*, INALCO, 2009.
5. Carpenter, E. S. *Eskimo Realities*, Holt Rinehart and Winston, 1973, p. 57.
6. Gombay, *op.cit.*

NANCY CAMPBELL
Houses look out over Disko Bay, in Ilulissat, Greenland.
Ilulissat means 'icebergs' in Kalaalissut.

LUCY ROSE KERR Home
White ink on black sugar paper
This is one of many meditative works I call 'Ghost Drawings'; images form on the page
unplanned, in response to music and contemplative thought. *Home* was a meditation
on a poem called 'Oath' by Jim Carter, and a soundtrack from the documentary *Cave
of Forgotten Dreams* by Werner Herzog.

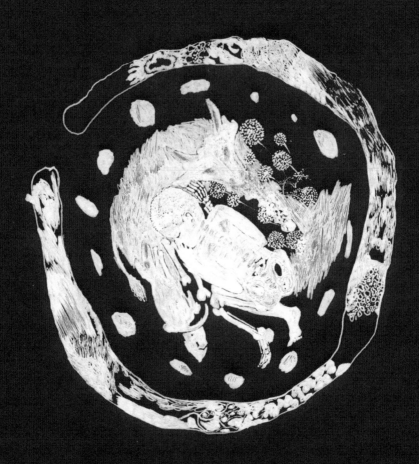

KATE WALTERS Creature Carrying Humans

Monotype with oil bar and ink

During last winter I spent six weeks working on the Isle of Iona. *The Bhagavad Gita* was a constant companion, as were Rilke's 'Duino Elegies'. I was particularly inspired by what Rilke explores in the 'Eighth Elegy': animals always being in the womb of creation. In this picture the Creature carries us all, in all our stages of imperfection.

CAROLINE DEAR Mantle *Dandelion*
One of a series of three full-size mantles, part of the exhibition 'Encircled by Gold'. This work was inspired by the archaeological site, High Pasture Cave or Uamh An Ard Achaidh, on Skye. This site has a record of human use since the Mesolithic 5000 BC, and it is where the body of an Iron Age woman was ceremonially buried. She was nicknamed Brigid by the archaeologists, the local area being Kilbride. She was laid on a bier with a mass of willow flowers and small amounts of red campion, white lily and holly flowers. These mantles were made using materials associated with St. Brigid and referencing her mantle of protection. This mantle is formed with rope made of dandelion stems and a hem made from bog cotton.

The Red Thread

> Women are imprisoned in the image masculine society has imposed on them; therefore if they attempt a free choice it must be a kind of gaolbreak.
> – Octavio Paz *(Labyrinth of Solitude)*

1962, London, England. *Give me my scallop-shell of quiet, / My staff of faith to walk upon, / My scrip of joy*

'Tell us about Raleigh!' we plead. We are in a history class, heathens all, in a dancing school in Knightsbridge. Lady Lisle takes off her pale blue glasses and flicks them in an agitated manner. She takes us to the Tower where the poet and New World adventurer is imprisoned for treason and recites the poem he writes before his execution. A tear falls down her wrinkled cheek.

Tell me the line of poetry you first remember and I will tell you about destiny.

THE THEME

The story of the Minotaur you know. Probably. Half-man, half-beast, he is kept in the centre of the Cretan Labyrinth, a prison system so complex it has even trapped its architect, Daedalus. No one who is sent into his Labyrinth gets out. The beast feeds on the flesh of young Athenians sent to him every seven years. Except for the hero Theseus, who has encountered the King of Crete's daughter, Ariadne. She has given him a thread, so that once he has vanquished the bull-man, he can find his way out again.

Ariadne will flee with Theseus to the island of Naxos and there the story ends. Usually. But in other versions it continues: Ariadne is abandoned by her lover on the shore, or her husband the half-god Dionysus reclaims her, or she hangs herself from a tree, or is killed by Artemis or Perseus, or is rescued from Hades by Dionysus, along with his mother Semele, or there are in fact two Ariadnes, one who dies and one who is immortal, and so on.

However you tell the story, Ariadne is a secondary player. She only knows the way out because she is the king's daughter. The red thread was bequeathed to her by Daedalus. She waits for the hero to do his heroic task and then disappears from view, leaving confusion in her wake.

But this is not the original version, where Ariadne commands the Labyrinth which is not a prison, but a map, named after her butterfly-shaped axe the *labrys*. To find that map, you would have to ask a poet. Because Ariadne's ur-story is not a story at all.

This is a short piece about poetry and its 'true function', which the poet Robert Graves famously described as religious invocation of the Muse, and a warning to man

> '…that he must keep in harmony with the family of living creatures among which he was born, by obedience to the wishes of the lady of the house.'

It is about the function of modern human beings, caught in the web of time, who try to find their way back home on Earth, out of the labyrinthine mind of civilisation, and what this has most urgently to do with the work and lives of poets. It's an instruction of sorts – though you might not read it that way.

THE MISTRESS OF THE LABYRINTH

She holds two snakes in her raised hands and wears a cat on her head like a bonnet. Discovered amongst the rubble at Knossos in 1904, the faience figurine was found in several pieces, and it was not clear whether the cat really belonged on her head. Still the Edwardian archaeologist placed it there instinctively, perhaps associating cats and female deities, as the well-catalogued civilisations along the Nile had shown him. He called this civilisation he unearthed 'Minoan' after Ariadne's father, King Minos.

Alongside the murals of dancing women and acrobatic men, red bulls and blue dolphins, she displays an elegance and fluidity unlike any found in later classical times. Sir Arthur Watts called her the Snake Priestess and sometimes Snake Goddess, though the highly organised culture she embodied left no evidence of temples, male hierarchy or stamp of war. It remains mysterious, its system of writing undeciphered to this day.

There is a fragment of a later script however that gives a clue:
To the Mistress of the Labyrinth, honey

This is a piece made of fragments. Of lines that pull you in different directions, flashes of memory and warning, threads poets leave behind to remind us that this world is not as it is made to appear.

THE FALL

When the world fell, the *yoginis* in the meditation chambers spoke to me in lines by Rilke and Rumi.

We shall not cease from exploration, they said.

When the world fell, the intellectuals in the libraries quoted lines to me by Blake and Brecht.

Things fall apart; the centre cannot hold, they said.

When the world fell, I fell with it. I was without lines for a long time. And then out of nowhere I began to remember:

My mother laughs. She comes bearing branches of hips and haws and a whiff of turpentine; parties follow in her wake, music and bright dresses.

There was once a path through the woods, she says.

My father sighs. He is writing into the night, stacking reams of legal papers, bound by pink ribbon, on his study floor:

I never saw a man who looked

    With such a wistful eye

Upon that little tent of blue

    Which prisoners call the sky

'Every time I pass through that prison gate, I shudder,' he tells me.

My teacher weeps. She laments the death of the Elizabethan poet, even more than the death of Jesus.

I don't trust those tears. I do not write *Tread softly for you tread on my dreams* on my rough book like my fellow pupils. I scorn romantics who worship queen and god and country, and love all dissenters and metaphysicians. The first poem I print with my own hands is in the shape of a butterfly:

Then shall the fall further the flight in me.

When you fall you don't find a new story or drama to live by. There are no tales when you are already at the ending. You grasp the thread because the line glints in that moment of darkness, like a coil of copper wire. It cuts you but still you take hold of it. Because it is the only thing that makes sense, as the world cracks you open. The line was written from the place of cracking – from the mad house and the gulag, from the dying rooms.

Eyeless in Gaza.

Only poetry speaks from this metaphysical realm. Novels with their worldly characters and clever entertaining plots, plays with their tragic and comedic turns: none of these serve you. In times of falling you won't remember those masterly passages that once gripped your attention. You can only a grab a line, and that line is no longer the literature that you once studied. It is not a comfort in a moment of self-pity or remorse.

It is something else.

THE CROSSING PLACE

1987, London, England. *Tonight I can write the saddest lines.* I am in your attic room under a mosquito net and the storm is rocking the capital. You are visiting a glamorous place, dressed in your black armour and war paint by Chanel.

Outside the wind is lashing the plane trees and the floor is covered in their leaves. My face is wet with rain. I don't know at this point that I will leave you and this city behind and never return. I don't know that years from now you will walk into the sea and not come back.

I have picked up a book by your bed but there is something hollow about these lines we used to read to each other. The poet will also put them away. I don't know that yet.

'My poetry stopped dead like a ghost in the streets of human anguish and a rush of roots and blood surged up through it,' he will write from war-torn Spain. 'From then on, my road meets everyman's road.'

1990, Palenque, Mexico. *Bid farewell to her, to Alexandria who is leaving. / Above all, do not delude yourself, do not say that it was a dream*

One bright morning, I followed the path through the woods that led away from the temple, and a man emerged naked from a pool. He said: *a queen swam here once* and gave me a jar of honey.

That night the forest came to our door and a jaguar lay down beside me. He watched an ancient civilisation rise and fall on the ceiling of our hotel room. I flew out on his eagle wings. I had to let everything go. There was nothing in the howling darkness that could take away the pain, or the poison that racked my body. *I am going*, he said, *but I am always here. Remember that.* I felt every bar that had shut down tight, pressed hard against my body, separating us. I realised I was trapped. Even my own name trapped me.

You realise everything up to that point was a rehearsal. That the real task was not finding the path you longed for, but the way out of the prison, where the gaoler lives inside you, and everyone else you meet.

1991, Antigua, Guatemala. *Pero yo ya no soy yo / Ni mi casa es ya mi casa.*

I am in another white room, only this time the storm is crashing through me. This time I am calling on it to do its ferocious work. Outside the world is coloured parrot green and pink. The volcanoes are snowy. The women laugh as they wash their clothes in the fountain.

There is a crisis point. You could call it 'the Theseus moment'. You were on your way to the Minotaur with your companions, brave Athenians all. You meet someone unexpected who hands you a red thread. When you stumble, you realise that thread you now hold to steady you does not come from any story you know.

There are no words to describe the feeling, as the forgotten files your education hid away, your culture hid away, stack up upon the cement floor. You cry out as you encounter this sunless place where your spirit has been locked up for aeons, where you have been kept in a small drawer, taken out occasionally to shine like a genie in a lamp. Where you pace like a creature in a trap, trying to find a way out.

The crossing lasts for days in the bare room, as you name every unkind thing that binds you. You are not the same person when you emerge finally into the sunlight. Your history is broken. The people who kept you captive are no longer with you.

You imagine that this is the end, when it is only the beginning.

Love is not servitude. This is what I learned in these encounters. It is neither obeisance to a moon goddess, nor enthrallment to a cruel queen. I knew that at eight years old. And yet to fall under your spell and break it was the way I could escape my own sacrifice. You were terrifying and captivating. You made everyone matter. You exuded the archetypal power of the Muse that Graves once wrote about: magnetic, intoxicated, sea-foamed, desirous of worship by poets and the hip bones of kings. But this power devoured you. In the end you wrote you were defeated by the struggle to stay alive. I looked back across time and saw you. You were like a lioness in a cage, maddened by captivity. The sea was your only escape.

Tonight I can write the saddest lines. But I am not going to. This is an instruction. This is not all there is.

THE RETURN

For a long time now I have wanted to write about the *Nostoi*, those who return to their homelands after the Trojan War. Return is not what you think it is, a glorious heroic odyssey full of wondrous islands, but the time when you know that we have all had our finest hour and we can no longer do to each other *what spring does to the cherry trees*. When the question becomes how to endure our fall as a people, how to keep our dignity, our sense of beauty, our capacity for intelligence and the strength and grace of our bodies, as the world crashes and the story we once believed in no longer makes sense.

What everyone avoids is feeling how that endless siege crippled us and trapped us in these thoughts. The terror comes when you sense the bars and know you no longer carry a sword. When you face the beast you will have nothing, except the very thing he wishes to devour.

If you hold fast this is the moment she appears in his blazing eye. Here she is with her laughter and her companions. Here they are in the alder grove, dancing in their beehive-shaped skirts, panels overlapping, with their bare feet on the earth.

Welcome, she says, to my dancing floor. The hard walls of the Labyrinth vanish and in its place are lines that loop around in an intricate pattern. They are of all colours and intersect in ways you can feel but cannot articulate. There is a hum you cannot tell whether is on the inside of you or the outside of you, it burns like a slow fire through your chest, and the scent of a thousand small flowers ...

'Focus,' she says, 'for this time is limited.'

'Oh, you are a bee!' I exclaim, 'And the bull is a star ...'

'This is your task,' she says. 'Find your way back.'

Because *I am with you in Rockland*

Because *Beloved be the one who sits down*

Because *Some people know what it is like to be called a cunt*
      in front of their children

Because *You took away all the oceans and all the room*

Because *Girls you are valuable, and you, Panther, you are valuable*

Because *The darkness around us is deep*

THE MINOTAUR

You think the Labyrinth is something you get free from, so you can live in the bright spaces. But that's not how it works. The volcano of Thera erupted and a tidal wave destroyed Europe's first civilisation, and it disappeared from view. Or so the archaeologists have told us. The Greek hero myths turned the great triple goddess of the matriarchal age into a foolish princess and started to straighten her looping songs and dances into linear, rational storylines.

The Labyrinth hid Ariadne's intricate dancing floor and her once-beloved bull became a child-eating monster. The patriarchal maze clung like a varroa mite on the back of a honeybee and infected the colonies of the Western world. Born configured still to dance and give honey, to love light and space and sea, we were confused by the dark place we now found ourselves in. Few of us remembered our way home.

And yet some of us cannot but attempt otherwise. The thread was put into our hands at the start.

The Minotaur waits in the Labyrinth, like Moloch, greedy for the flesh of young men and woman, sucking the minds and hearts of all who sacrifice their youth, their brilliance, their sacred groves, their own offspring. This place is powered by his appetite.

How do I know this? I am my Mother's daughter, a child of space and air, who loved to dance, to go for a picnic on a summer's day. Who still goes for a picnic on a summer's day, with the sound of the sea in the distance. But I am my Father's daughter first, indentured, duty-bound, to live another kind of life. While my playmates listened to children's stories, he instructed me: on how the Bastille was liberated, how to decipher a brief, how to look for the detail in everything and outwit everyone in the court, cleverly with words.

At night I would hear him tap-tap-tapping into the small hours, fighting to keep a man or woman out of the prison he feared. Only writers know this kind of deal: you get to glimpse the paradise in everything and you get to feel the hell of everything. You work to bring back Ariadne's dancing floor by deconstructing the Labyrinth. It is the deal that drives poets crazy on the top of mountains, and sometimes costs them their lives, their sanity and their liberty.

For prose writers 'poetic' is an insult word. It means you are foolish and flowery and none of your arguments stand up in the witness box. But it is hard not to write about the beauty of the house. Even now I am trying to find a way to not get beautiful, not tell you about the colours of the garden; these roses that will become my mother's hips in September, and the bees that cluster about the clover leys, the sound of the wren singing, the way the wind moves through the barley and wild grasses in late June.

The poet loves beauty but is condemned to write about the Labyrinth and shake all who read his lines. Here he comes with his window of blue sky, with his words that break down the door, between the city and the forest, between politeness and reality. Here she is tapping a code that you work hard to decipher in your solitary cell, scraping a tunnel underneath your feet, leaving graffiti in her wake on the stony wall.

Here they are with their access to realms you cannot see but sometimes sense, swinging between history and myth, between life and death, only listened to, like gods, in moments of fall and destruction.

I am not a poet. I am condemned to write prose, urgent pleas to reverse your sentence.

A Daedalus daughter, unwinged.

2004, Aldeburgh, Suffolk. *Times are bad. I take an oath of loyalty to the table / coated with white Formica.*

'No one wants to know about the Wall, Charlotte,' said Aharon Shabtai, as we stood balancing glasses of wine and plates of salad at the festival reception. That afternoon the Israeli poet had thrown down his poems mid-sentence, smashing the wall that separated him from the audience. He spoke about the wall that is being built to separate the Arabs and the Jews of his country. 'You have to hear this!' he cried.

Everyone clapped politely: 'How dreadful!' they agreed, as they sat in their neatly pressed clothes, as the wind screamed past the church hall and over the bay, where 200 years ago one of the most anguished figures of English poetry pointed his fishing boat towards the horizon.

I live in George Crabbe country now, a flat, salty place where I have learned to wear a shabby coat and live among the lowly and dispossessed, the small weeds crushed underfoot he once catalogued in his unfashionable heroic style. I know we can't afford to be romantic anymore. To get out of the Labyrinth is our most urgent task.

2016, Ipswich, Suffolk. *Neither father nor mother, nor any playmate; / Only an avenue, dark, nameless, without end*

There are soldiers everywhere on the platform, dressed in wool khaki. 'What are you doing here?' I ask one of them. The boy gazes into my eyes and something like terror and grief jolts through me. He hands me a card that reads: *Rifleman R.G. Cole. London Regiment (Queen Victoria's Rifles).*

'Oh,' I say, 'you cannot speak!' I don't know it yet but this is a performance being acted out in railway stations all over Britain to mark the Battle of the Somme. It is a show, except it does not feel like one.

In the carriage the ghost riflemen sit silently among the passengers. Opposite me the poet Luke Wright, famous for his rollicking political satire, looks up from his computer screen and watches them.

A hundred years ago on this day 19,240 young men from Britain died in a war that is remembered as much for its poetry as for its bloody sacrifice. Thousands from the small villages of Suffolk boarded the trains to France and did not return. You can still feel their absence in the fields when you go walking. Loss is not a personal matter anymore. I have learned that too in these sandy waterlands, where time becomes unmoored.

I look at the card in my hands and shudder: *we are here*, it says.

This is an instruction. The way back is hard. It is populated by the dead, the ones you know and the ones you don't, and you cannot be afraid of them. You cannot be afraid of the unconscious that craves to devour the heart and the light that lives inside you. Your journey liberates them, as much as it liberates you.

Return does not mean back in time as you understand it, along the linear lines of story. It means we return to a place of feeling and spirit, untrammelled by war and hierarchy, even if it takes us aeons to get there. Poets hold the fragments of that place inside them, as they have always held the line, a long line that stretches back to a time where there were no fortresses or prisons, when the bull was not a beast.

The Labyrinth traps us in history, and keeps us from the dancing floor. We have to remember that as Western people, as people born in captivity. We have to know we were not abandoned.

Her threads are everywhere.

With thanks: Sir Walter Raleigh, Robert Graves, Pablo Neruda, Federico García Lorca, C. P. Cavafy, T. S. Eliot, W. B. Yeats, Rudyard Kipling, Oscar Wilde, George Herbert, John Milton, Allen Ginsberg, César Vallejo, Rita Ann Higgins, Osip Mandlestam, Stevie Smith, William Stafford, Aharon Shabtai, George Crabbe, Edward Thomas.

231

I Have No Problem

Mourid Barghouti

I look at myself:
I have no problem.
I look all right
and, to some girls,
my grey hair might even be attractive;
my eyeglasses are well made,
my body temperature is precisely thirty seven,
my shirt is ironed and my shoes do not hurt.
I have no problem.

My hands are not cuffed,
my tongue has not been silenced yet,
I have not, so far, been sentenced
and I have not been fired from my work;
I am allowed to visit my relatives in jail,
I'm allowed to visit some of their graves in some countries.
I have no problem.

I am not shocked that my friend
has grown a horn on his head.
I like his cleverness in hiding the obvious tail
under his clothes,

لا مُشْكِلَة لَدَيَّ

أتَلَمَّسُ أحوالي...
لا مشكلة لديَّ

شكلي مقبولٌ. ولبعض الفتيات
أبدو بالشعر الأبيض جذاباً
نظّاراتي متقنة
وحرارةُ جسمي سبعٌ وثلاثونَ تماماً
وقميصي مكويٌّ وحذائي لا يؤلمني
لا مشكلة لدي

كَفّاي بلا قَيْدٍ. ولساني لم يُسكَتْ بعد
لم يصدر ضدي حُكْمٌ حتى الآن
ولم أطرَدْ مِن عملي
مسموحٌ لي بزيارةِ مَن سَجَنوهمْ مِن أهلي
وزيارةِ بعض مقابرهمْ، في بعض البلدان
لا مشكلة لدي

لا يدهشني أن صديقي أنْبَتَ قَرْناً في رأسه
وأُحِبُّ بَراعَتَهُ في إخفاء الذيل الواضح تحت ملابسِهِ
وهدوءُ مخالِيهِ يُعجبني.
قد يفتك بي، لكني سوف أسامحه

233

I like his calm paws.
He might kill me, but I shall forgive him
for he is my friend;
he can hurt me every now and then.
I have no problem.

The smile of the TV anchor
does not make me ill any more
and I've got used to the Khaki stopping my colours
night and day.
That is why
I keep my identification papers on me, even at the swimming pool.
I have no problem.

Yesterday, my dreams took the night train
and I did not know how to say good bye to them.
I heard the train has crashed
in a barren valley
(only the driver survived).
I thanked God, and took it easy
for I have small nightmares
that I hope will develop into great dreams.
I have no problem.

I look at myself, from the day I was born till now.
In my despair I remember

فهو صديقي
وله أن يؤذيني أحيانًا
لا مشكلة لدي

ما عادت بسمات مذيع التلفزيون
تُسبِّبُ لي أمراضًا.
وتعوَّدت على توقيف الكاكيِّين لألواني
ليلًا ونهارًا. ولهذا
أحمِلُ أوراقي الشخصية حتى في المَسْبَح
لا مشكلة لدي

أحلامي رَكِبَتْ، أمس، قِطارَ الليل
ولم أعرف كيف أودعها
وأنتثني أنباءُ تَدَهْوُرِهِ في وادٍ ليس بذي زرع
(ونجا سائقه من بين الركاب جميعًا)
فحمدت الله، ولم أبكِ كثيرًا
فلديَّ كوابيسٌ صغرى
سأطوّرها، إن شاء الله، إلى أحلام كبرى
لا مشكلة لدي

أتلمَّس أحوالي منذ وُلدتُ إلى اليوم
وفي يأسي أتذكر

that there is life after death;
there is life after death
and I have no problem.

But I ask:
Oh my God,
is there life *before* death?

أن هناك حياةٌ بعد الموتِ
هناك حياة بعد الموت
ولا مشكلة لدي

لكني أسأل:
يا الله!
أهناك حياةٌ "قَبْلَ" المَوْت؟

Mala Memoria

La historia es una ciencia
que se funda en la mala memoria
  – Miroslav Holub

Cuando llegaron las primeras lluvias
    hicimos lo necesario:
    bajamos de nuestros altos pensamientos
    y comenzamos a labrar los campos;
    las manos eran nuestras palas
    los pies eran nuestros pies
    y regamos la semilla
    con nuestras lágrimas

Luego vinieron los sacerdotes
    envueltos en grandes plumas amarillas
    y palabras más brillantes que el mar;
    hablaron con imágenes
    y también para ellos
    hicimos lo que era necesario:

Poor Memory

(transl. Mark Schafer)

History is a science
based on poor memory
  – Miroslav Holub

When the first rains fell
    we did what was necessary:
    we climbed down from our lofty thoughts
    and began to work the fields;
    our hands served as shovels
    our feet served as feet
    and we watered the seeds
    with our tears

Then came the priests
    wrapped in great yellow feathers
    and words more dazzling than the sea;
    they spoke in images
    and we did what was necessary
    for them as well:

Construimos una carretera larga
    muy larga
    una carretera larguísima
    que va desde la casa de los muertos
    hasta la casa de los que van a morir

Entonces aparecieron las nubes
    sobre el río redondo
    y escuchamos voces
    que hacían trizas nuestras vocales;
    comprendimos que el final estaba cerca

Hicimos lo necesario:
    extendimos nuestras pocas pertenencias
    y fingimos que ya lo sabíamos todo;
    aprendimos a llorar
    como las mujeres y los niños
    y los niños y las mujeres
    aprendieron a mentir como los hombres

Tres grandes agujeros se abrieron en el cielo:
    por el primero descendió la luna
    por el segundo ascendió la serpiente
    y por el tercero bajó una estrella de hojalata;
    cuando tocó la tierra
    supimos que el tiempo era cumplido

We built a long highway
　　very long
　　a very, very long highway
　　leading from the house of the dead
　　to the house of those who are going to die

Then the clouds appeared
　　over the round river
　　and we heard voices
　　that smashed our vowels to pieces;
　　we knew the end was near

We did what was necessary:
　　we spread out our few belongings
　　and pretended we knew it all;
　　we learned to cry
　　like women and children
　　and the children and women
　　learned to lie like men

Three large holes opened in the sky:
　　the moon dropped through the first
　　the serpent rose through the second
　　and a tin star descended through the third;
　　when it touched ground
　　we knew the time was at hand

Hicimos lo necesario:

  desgarramos el velo

  y batimos el tambor

  hasta que el vacío

  se instaló en nuestros corazones;

  un rostro desconocido apareció

  en los intersticios de la tela

  y cuando sus labios se movieron

  un nuevo espacio surgió frente a nosotros

Hicimos lo necesario:

  tomamos las montañas

  y las pusimos bocabajo

  para que pudieran recuperar el aliento;

  tomamos los ríos

  y los pusimos de pie

  para que volvieran a ver el cielo;

  luego tomamos nuestros cuerpos

  por la punta de las alas

  y los fuimos a lavar en el espejo de los nombres

Fue entonces cuando nos dieron la orden de despertar

  e hicimos lo necesario:

  atrás quedaron los campos

  y las campanas manchadas

  por el canto de un pájaro del otro mundo;

We did what was necessary:
    we rent our veils
    and beat on our drums
    until the void
    lodged in our hearts;
    an unfamiliar face appeared
    through the rifts of the fabric
    and when its lips moved
    an unfamiliar space materialised before us

We did what was necessary
    we took the mountains
    and turned them upside down
    so they could catch their breath;
    we took the rivers
    and stood them up
    so they could see the sky again;
    then holding our bodies
    by the tips of our wings
    we washed them in the mirror of names

That's when they commanded us to wake up
    and we did what was necessary:
    we left the fields behind
    and the bells strained
    by the song of a bird from another world;

atrás quedaron también los mapas
preparados para la huida
y no nos quedó más remedio
que seguir adelante sin mapas
que es lo mismo
que quedarse

Vimos venir desde el fondo de la tierra
un sordo rumor
un torbellino de nada
con un viento recién nacido
entre las manos:
la criatura nos dijo
lo que siempre hemos querido saber
y siempre olvidamos:
que no hay más sueño que éste
y que despertar es otro sueño
más profundo
si despertamos para adentro
o más superficial
si despertamos para afuera

Como no supimos cuál era cuál
hicimos lo necesario:
nos sentamos a esperar
el derrumbe

we also left behind the maps
prepared for our flight
and there was nothing for us to do
but go on without maps
which is the same
as staying put

We watched as from the depths of the earth
a low murmur approached
a whirlwind of nothing
a new-born gust
in its hands:
the creature told us
what we have always wanted to know
and always forget:
that this is the only dream
and that awakening is another dream
deeper
if we wake inward
or more superficial
if we wake outward

Since we couldn't tell which was which
we did what was necessary:
we sat down to wait
for the collapse

Y seguimos esperando...

Como si esperar
    no fuera suficiente trabajo

And we are still waiting...

As if waiting
      weren't hard enough

Roots in Stone

Neale Jones

...there is relief and freedom in knowing what is real...To
flee from its realities is only to arrive at them unprepared.
– Wendell Berry

Park at the edge of the winding road, its cracked asphalt, beside the
line of thick-trunked eucalyptus. Leave the car, close the door. Feel
the wind off the sea, smell the salt spray, hear the soughing of the
sickle-like eucalyptus leaves, the broad planes of coast cypress. The
thunder of the surf falling upon the granite teeth of the coast.

Behind the eucalyptus trees rises the mortared stone of a house
wall, a garage door, little windows. It might appear, at a glance, that
this is the exterior of one of the mansions that now populate this
headland by Carmel Bay. But something about it feels less refined,
less precise and industrial. Perhaps it is the crumbling surfaces of the
granite boulders, their organic shapes and variable size, no facade.
Perhaps it is the wooden frames of the windows, their palm-sized
panes, the suggestion that something as common as glass is precious.

And here is a boulder beside the wheel of your car, with a bronze
plaque showing the names: *Robinson Jeffers, Tor House.*

Turn down the flagstone drive beyond the boulder. Now you can
see the stone garden wall, the herb shrubs waving in the wind.
Further on, the low cottage with its shallow sloping roof, the later
additions to the house winding back toward the road. And standing
apart from the rest of the rambling compound, the promontory
upthrust that is Hawk Tower, shadowed, backlit by the clouds over
the Pacific, white light through its window like a beacon.

Step through the garden gate. Remark upon the broken tile set into the mortar of the wall, a shard from a Chinese temple. A discarded grave marker makes a flagstone in the path. A sense of the sacred, not as distinct from, but integrated into something as quotidian as a wall, or a path.

Walk down that path. Hear the gulls cry, see them ride the wind. Smell the sagebrush, woody and acrid, its small hard leaves. Kneel down amidst the shrubs and small flowers, work your fingers into a bare patch of soil. Bring them out oily and black, holding the broken shard of an abalone shell. This sloping knoll is a midden, left here by the people native to this coast, the Ohlone. Over thousands of years, their discarded shells and the charcoal from their fires mounded up here. This hill remains as evidence of a life integrated with the land, of the continuity of that life through long time. The trees, the sage-brush and the house, they all have their roots in this midden.

Stand with the soot still on your hand. Go on down the path, to the door of the cottage. Here you can see the grain of the granite in the walls, the crystals exposed by the wear of salt and ocean wave. This upright structure was built by people – at once the weathered stone has the appearance of geology, of a glacial moraine.

Likewise raw is the dark wood of the door. The iron handle and keyhole showing rust and also the oiled sheen of use. It is clear these things, the walls, the door, the handle, were made by hand, for this place in particular. Put the large key in the hole, feel the hardy mech-anism turn over. Step inside.

Here you find a parlour, panelled in old redwood, stained by time to the colour of ox blood. The ceiling beams, bare and solid, rest low. The furniture is short-legged, nestled in the corners or beside the hearth of rough granite. Benches line a corner around a little piano, beneath windows of the familiar small panes, which look out to the breakers riding in, the line of the horizon where grey ocean meets paler sky. In this small room, its wood close and warm and dark, there is the sense of being held, contained within, as in an animal den.

Sit on a bench by the window. Take in the browned family photos, the soot still blackening the fireplace. The light from the clouds that angles through the window's many panes. Sit and listen to this poem.

*

Robinson Jeffers came to this place in 1914, with his new wife Una. He was an unknown poet. This was a windswept headland, bereft of trees or homes. Standing here and looking south they would have been met by the wild Big Sur coast, where the rugged Santa Lucia mountains face directly the massed violence of the Pacific Ocean.

If you come to the Big Sur country, now often called Jeffers Country, you will see this: knife-edge ridges diving into roiling surf, deep-riven gorges crossed by spindly bridges, wind-tortured redwoods clinging to the mountaintops and looking out to the inconceivable vastness of the Pacific, clouds greater than any mountain riding stately gales on that horizon, the sun lancing through them, pillared on the shining mirror of the fractured ocean. You will see hawks and vultures haunting the hard sea wind, pelicans and gulls and cormorants skimming over the swells. You may see the shy deer in the shadows of inland redwood groves, or rattlesnakes coiled in the stones below bare peaks. You will see fissured granite islands breaking the waves to foam and ice-blue water, you will see kelp waving in the rushing surf, otters and seals riding through it unperturbed. You will see the great stone prow of Point Lobos, haggard cypresses on its foredeck, facing into the unrelenting ferocity rolling in from the west.

If you were here with Jeffers when he first came to this place, you would also have seen a few people, going about their lives amidst all this intensity and grandeur. You would have seen what he saw:

... people living – amid magnificent unspoiled scenery – essentially as they did in the Idyls or the Sagas, or in Homer's Ithaca. Here was life purged of its ephemeral accretions. Men were riding after cattle, or plowing the headland, hovered by white sea-gulls, as they have done for thousands of years, and will for thousands of years to come. Here was contemporary life that was also permanent life; and not shut from the modern world but conscious of it and related to it; capable of expressing its spirit, but unencumbered by the mass of poetically irrelevant details and complexities that make a civilization.[1]

*

I grew up not far from here, but had never heard of Jeffers or his house. His work was assigned in a community college class on local literature, and I bought the small used paperback along with the stack of other books. The charcoal drawing of his face on the cover, the pages yellowing and coarse-fibered.

When I began to read, I heard a clear voice, emphatic, ringing. A message I had heard nowhere else as distinctly, that meaning is found in the terrible beauty of the greater cosmos, not in the insular human, and that that meaning and beauty come from the extremity of being, the strain to live our small increment.

*

I came upon Jeffers at an appropriate time. While I parsed his lines and wrote papers about him, a friend of mine lay sick with cancer. A close friend, and one my own age, barely twenty. The cancer was a rare type, untreatable, metastasising through his liver, his joints.

I visited him often in the hospital, went home to continue my education. Between these colliding worlds, between the smell of anti-septic floors and the classroom's mouldering carpet, between the snaking tubes from bags of fluid and the shuffling line to the bursar's payment window, I read Jeffers and walked by the shore, watched the great waves roll in. I heard him say, *This coast crying out for tragedy like all beautiful places: / and like the passionate spirit of humanity / Pain for its bread ...* [2]

I was shaken awake into raw grief. Like birth, the rudest awakening, emerging into a world where everything seemed imbued with pain. But also like drawing a first breath, a sense at last of being touched by the real.

*

Jeffers too would be shaken awake. By the Big Sur country, its undeniable power. And by the Great War, its immensity of human tragedy. At the close of that chapter of trauma, as the Armistice came about, he and Una bought their acres of headland beside Carmel Bay, and began to build Tor House.

It was only to be a small cottage at first, built of the granite boulders the waves carved out of their shore, of the redwood that grew tall in the protected gorges of Big Sur. The house would be spare and contained, just a few rooms lacking running water, lit by oil lamps, heated by the small hearth. Already they were working under this ethos they had seen expressed in the land and people, permanent life persisting by emphasising basic needs, eschewing civilisation's confusing accretions. A focus on the real, the durable and the reoccurring, as opposed to the unreal lightning flashes of thoughts and wants that make up so much of our culture.

For the building of the cottage they employed local labourers and contractors. The story goes that Jeffers was impatient to see the structure finished, and apprenticed himself to the stonemason to speed the construction.* I have to suspect, given his appreciation for stone in his poetic work, that there must have been another motivation, beyond mere efficiency. Rather than be a bystander, he wanted to be deeply entwined with what would become their home for the rest of their lives. To stand back and pay others to build for you, that is an act of disconnection. To work toward the building of your own house, hauling the stones up from the tide-line, the westering sun and the salt spray on your skin, to heave the stones up and place them where they lie even and stable in the walls, learning the ways of granite, *the art to make stone love stone*[3] – this is connection.

*

I watched my friend being worn away by cancer. It was becoming clear that none of us are safe. There is this narrative to which we Americans subscribe: grow up do your homework go to college get a job go to the gym don't smoke eat right get married have some kids teach them to do the same everything will be fine you'll never die. This terrible and bald lie, immediately ruined by my friend reaching for me with his withered arm, unable to rise from the bed.

We had played music together for years. We laughed into the witching hours. We were within a year in age. Then he became sick, and he fell into a coma that lasted a month.

When he came awake, he had aged beyond me. His body was suddenly old, death coming close. He had leapt a gap we think ought to be filled with an almost endless swathe of time. It is the kind of advanced age you can recognise in the eyes.

* For some details of Jeffers' story, I have relied on descriptions by the docents at Tor House.

A distance growing between us. He, dissolving into the greater world. I, trapped in a prison of the mind.

He died in the summer. I was away on a trip in a mountain wilderness. I felt him go, an anguish of grief, something torn up at the roots. At that moment, I didn't know the reason. When I returned home, he had already gone, the memorial had been held. Then I found out the day and the time, knew I had felt him dying. Through that pain we had touched each other.

*

In the Big Sur landscape, Jeffers found his great teacher: nature unadorned, lacking all human affectation. He could have sought a philosophy in the accumulations of civilisation, in its literature and religion, its essentially human concerns. Instead, he walked out into the Big Sur country. There was Pico Blanco, a *steep sea-wave of marble*,[4] ragged Point Lobos *the gaunt cypresses crown*,[5] the unending rhythm of waves eating rock, steadily destroying the continent. Like a wilderness prophet he went beyond the pale, into the uncontrolled land. From it he took his doctrine of the real, of the perdurable, of raw and unbridled beauty.

In that place he found kinship, with hawks and granite stones. He saw how utterly impossible it is to dissever ourselves from the life of the greater world, any more than might a hawk or stone. And looking back from that place, north toward the cities of Monterey and San Francisco, with those hawk's eyes, how clearly petty and ephemeral they would have seemed, a fiction of human independence and separateness.

*

I was unprepared for true grief. It is civilised to view death and pain as failures. Death by cancer in particular, which is seen as needless and random, something we have to wage war upon. We don't want to prepare ourselves. Technology will soon make it unnecessary.

We seem to think death and pain themselves must somehow be vulnerable to this technological war. Someday, progress will have taken care of these problems that beset us. Anything uncomfortable will be done away with.

That's the implicit promise. So we outsource the functional work of caring for the sick, the dying, the bodies of the dead. We avoid in particular the terminally ill, as if the taint of death could rub off on us. We will never see a dead body, aside from a mannequin in an open casket.

Never mind that these moments might serve, among other things, as a way to acknowledge reality, to step into necessary grief. That would allow for a discomfort deep and real.

*

I had no form for this grief, no dance in which to place my steps. There was no plan for this, no preparation. A dissonance in myself. Everything wrong and no help. The old religions and the new age both saying there was a loving deity with a plan. Materialist science plugging its ears and humming to ignore the failure, seeking answers in minutia, atheism closing in on solipsism, the thoughts in the head. In that same period came the trauma of terrorist attack, followed by the clangour of jingoism. Wars on cancer, wars on nations. Capital and technology, thrown without cease after ultimate waste, pain and destruction. Chemo and carpet bombs. Terror, and no place for a feeling body to live.

What deity would make it this way? What could allow for this?

Seeking escape from this strain, I went to the shore. I went south and sat on the rocks below Tor House. I watched the waves come in endlessly from the west, throw themselves on the rocks to be destroyed. I watched the rocks breaking up through the flowing surf, steadily eaten away in their turn.

At least there was a place for this feeling, intense and raw, like a torn wound inside, but so large it seemed to go beyond me. If I had to feel it, here was the place, where the Pacific Ocean claws at the feet of the Santa Lucia.

The anguish was greater than me, of course it was. It is as large as the cosmos, everything that is. It is the feeling of everything being torn apart, the price of being. There was never another plan.

*

In his work on Tor House, Jeffers had discovered a twin passion to poetry: building with stone. It wasn't long before he undertook new building projects by himself. First a garden wall to contain the children, followed by a garage for the family Model A.

Having refined his skills, he soon broke ground on the project of Hawk Tower. It was intended more for Una, a gesture toward the Irish towers she loved. The body of the tower contains boulders weighing as much as four hundred pounds. Jeffers raised them using a makeshift pulley system and scaffold, setting them in place by hand. It would take six years to complete.

During this time, Jeffers began a routine he would continue for most of his life: writing in the morning, at a small desk in the upper story of the cottage, and building or tree-planting in the afternoon. He would eventually plant as many as two thousand trees along that headland, mostly coast cypress and eucalyptus. They became his *planted forest,*[6] a kind of screen between the Jeffers homestead and the civilisation that was already beginning to encroach.

Outdoor work, with trees and stones, and crafting poetry were Jeffers' daily occupations. That they engaged equal portions of his time is not an accident. Already it was becoming clear that both life and art ought to be concerned with the durable. Jeffers expected his trees to outlast him, so with the house and its tower, so with his poetry. The most valuable things, in poetry and the broader world, were those that persist, perhaps for thousands of years:

> Permanent things, or things forever renewed, like the grass and human passions, are the material for poetry; and whoever speaks across the gap of a thousand years will understand that he has to speak of permanent things, and rather clearly...[7]

The durable and perdurable, the stolid mountain and reoccurring human feeling, have greater meaning in their ever-returning cycles. The atomised and self-important human is lost to that.

In his poems Jeffers speaks to the land, the sea, the night, the house and the stones that will lie in its walls. While others might see them as inert material, he recognises their broader life beyond their utility for him. He knows they feel in their own way, have their own experience. That is their purpose – not to build him a house, though *this [is] also destined*.[8] Tor House is alive the way the land is alive, and the house and Jeffers' oeuvre grow from the same root: the need to live close to the raw life of the world.

Little house, he writes to the cottage, *each stone / Baptized from that abysmal font / The sea and the secret earth gave bonds to affirm you*.[9] Even as he uses the diminutive *little*, bringing the house close like a child, with all the warmth and connection that entails, he baptises it in the molten heart-blood of the earth, the endless violence of the ocean waves. Even as he builds the house for protection, he brings the unrestrained upheaval of the world close at hand, and both building the house and writing his poetry become primeval ritual.

*

Jeffers had something of a crisis at the outset of his poetic career, when he realised how little he had to show for his work – he was well aware of what Pound and Eliot had already achieved. He had the education to follow them down what he called their *narrowing lane*[10] – highly allusive, using the imagery of civilisation as a cypher to describe the internal landscape, *abstract, unreal, eccentric*[11] – but he felt that *every advance required the elimination of some aspect of reality*[12]. At the end was a meaningless virtuosity.

The Modernists were too civilised for Jeffers – they remained trapped in human solipsism. Within the sphere of civilisation, allusion eventually becomes self-reference. And just as civilisation implies the urban, *the life of modern cities [is] barren of poetry; it is not a lasting life; and it is lived among unrealities.*[13] These unrealities compound and compound in a feedback loop, transient human wants looming large in our view, disallowing contemplation of our small place in a greater cosmos. The high achievements of civilisation to which we might refer, whether the glittering cityscapes or the highly refined technique of Modernist poetry, in the broader view are revealed as ephemeral and hollow, towers of glass.

*

Other deaths would haunt me as time went on.

A childhood friend developed schizophrenia, was put on antipsychotic drugs. A short time later she died in a fall from a seaside cliff. An accident, or a suicide, some slippage between the two, we don't know.

This coast crying out for tragedy like all beautiful places...[14]

I made a friend in a fiction writing class at community college. He and I exchanged writing, we had a rapport that way. He was quiet, discerning in critique. He was sometimes hard to read. He didn't tell me that his wife had left him for his best friend. Instead he took a gun, and killed his best friend and then himself.

We sooner more liable / Than the other animals. Pain and terror, the insanities of desire...[15]

My grandmother was struck suddenly by a stroke. She lived and was conscious for a few more months, but soon she drew back into herself, all energy in the body straining to continue. I sang to her as she died in the hospital room.

...not accidents but essential...[16]

My wife got a call and she gasped and cried, *My dad is dead!*

He had been on a backpacking trip in the dry wilderness of the Big Sur coast. A year of drought and fires.

Beautiful country burn again... Burn as before with bitter wonders...[17]

He hadn't had enough water with him. He probably suffered from heatstroke, on a narrow path above one of the Santa Lucia's deep ravines. He slipped and fell far down the rocky slope – he died before anyone could reach him.

A terrible, appropriate coincidence. As if the Big Sur country had claimed another sacrifice.

It was not much later that my marriage died. As though a person had been born between us, the relationship became a living thing that grew, then sickened. Over and over, my wife fell in love with other men. I stayed in our small apartment with the dog, surrounded by the San Francisco fog, crushed by loneliness.

There were times when I felt rage enough to do violence. That she, who I had trusted, could choose to hurt me so much. I was stripped bare, all raw feeling, primal urges near the surface. The steady dawning of a grief over the dying dreams, the decaying image of my life.

*

An ultimate loneliness in me. That if everyone will be lost in death, could disappear at any time, there is a profound emptiness at the heart of things, where everyone had said there ought to be a loving God.

I went to Jeffers Country more often. I sat below his house, looked up at the tower against the pale sky. I hiked into the back-country of Big Sur, wandered among the cypresses of Point Lobos. And I sought out other wild places, the crags of the high Sierra Nevada, the alpine meadows of the Marble Mountains.

There I felt an expansiveness, where there was room for grief and pain. There was ecstatic joy too, watching the maned breakers sweep in, or the spouts of whales in their pods, or a bear meandering in the mountain dawn. This was different than the constrained pathways I walked in the cities, the sense that all this feeling was covered over by concrete, the real hidden away.

A dead world is one where we are doomed to suffer our humanity confined to our skulls. Prisoners of our insular perspective. That is a world where suicide is the only logical course.

Among the wild non-human, the idea that we are the only things that feel became a clear fallacy to me, replaced by a recognition in my guts that I was part of a feeling cosmos, one particle humming with pain and ecstasy along with all the rest. In place of that civilised self-involvement I found myself enmeshed in the body of a self-torturing universe, everything around me aching with beauty.

Jeffers gives voice to this universal deity, who, like Odin hanging from his tree, sacrifices the pain of being for the sake of discovery. *Each moment of being is new,* it says, *therefore I still refrain my burning / thirst from the crystal-black / Water of an end.*[18]

The pain was not reduced by knowing it was felt by a greater being. Only I knew I could endure it, and there was a real purpose. And that I was not alone.

*

Jeffers' work is defined in large part by his long narrative poems. In them he transports the violent imagery of Greek tragedies to the Big Sur landscape, as human obsessions lead to rape, incest, maiming, self-mutilation, suicide, insanity, murder of all kinds. The criticism is that its purpose is mere pornographic shock, facile allusion.

But Jeffers has a purpose beyond the lurid or referential. He is not trying to allude so much as remake.

Before they were written down, the ancient Greek stories were an oral tradition, meant as both entertainment and a conveyance of cultural knowledge. Like those ancient poets, Jeffers is making epics for his own time, embedded in the landscape of Big Sur. And like those Greek tragedians, Jeffers sees hubris as an essential concept. Though our contemporary culture owes much to ancient Greece, we seem not to have learned this emphatic lesson: whoever thinks of himself as centrally important will come to ruin.

In modernity we take an anthropological or literary view of the Greek gods and heroes, always from the stance that we are more reasonable now. We see belief in those gods as, at base, a superstition.

The pantheon arrived with the Greeks from pre-literate times, however. They are not so much gods of the book, but of the landscape. They are closely tied to non-human natural forces, and their capriciousness and implacability mirror those forces. They might be said to be direct, animistic naming of the deep power of sea and storm, blazing sun, fecund earth, growing things, cycles of order and entropy.

In that frame, stories of hubris don't depict rebellion against an imaginary overlord, but incite us to recognise our small place amidst a massive natural world. An inflated sense of self-importance can only lead to woe, as one goes in opposition to those titanic forces.

Jeffers needs the shock of violence more than ever in this age, when hubris is the conventional mode. In Jeffers' time and ours, humanity would believe it has conquered the world – an ancient Greek would have recognised that as sophistry. The incredible power of the churning cycles of nature are evident in Big Sur, the violent rending and remaking of land and sea – in a reversal of the Greek personification of those massive powers, Jeffers brings that violence into the human scale.

*

The violence and death in my own life could have been the fodder for one of Jeffers' narrative poems. Some might say he is too morbid, too lurid, but I say those things were in my life. And my life is not exceptional.

Our civilisation would like to turn away from this grief. From acknowledging the pain of existence. We would like to bury the trauma, believe that things will never fall apart. With each new catastrophe we are unprepared, we have to convince ourselves that it's outside the norm. We have to anesthetise ourselves, become once again amnesiac.

Like Jeffers, I couldn't turn away. I had to feel. An iota of that greater feeling, the world spinning through its black night. As Jeffers says, poetry is *not a refuge but an incitement.*[19] Poetry's purpose is to reveal the beauty of the real. That beauty comes from enduring the pain of being.

*

There was a lapse in my personal griefs, for some time I lost no one. But in that place was a growing realisation of the damage being done to the non-human, the assault on the beauty of the world. The metastasising concrete, the only-human landscape. *Mind like a many-bladed machine,* Jeffers says, *subduing the / world with deep indifference.*[20]

Throughout California, there were wildfires and drought. The snowpack in the Sierra Nevada was perpetually low, ski resorts blowing artificial snow onto the slopes. Across the Santa Lucia Range from the Big Sur Coast lies the Central Valley, once one of the richest wetlands in the world. The valley floor was sinking as its water was sucked up into citrus and nut trees, exported. Civilisation eats California. Farmers were drilling new wells.

The people beseeched the weather like a mechanistic god, playing a slot machine, hoping for a jackpot of rain, so they could go on as before.

Jeffers' words:

> Broad wagons before sunrise bring food into the city from
> the open farms,
> > and the people are fed.
> They import and they consume reality. Before sunrise a hawk
> in the desert
> > made them their thoughts.[21]

*

Jeffers has been forgotten because he was one of civilisation's most ardent critics. He saw it as a *mass of poetically irrelevant details and complexities.*[22] The poetically relevant is the meaningful beauty of the world, beauty through endurance, and the things that endure are the most real.

Civilisation consumes reality, the way that it consumes California. The real things of the world – land and ocean, the mountain's ragged peak, the ever-returning waves of grass, the long-lived trees, the soil and the food that grows from it – these we commodify and consume, wrapped in the ephemeral – packaging, marketing, media, industrial processes. For lithe and wild fish, we have a fillet under plastic, for trees we have 'standing timber' or lumber in the yard. For nature, we have programming. Civilisation has convinced us we can't live without it, and even further that it *is* life. To accomplish this it must always distort, process, keep at bay the real.

Civilisation is a belief in only ourselves. Like the sufferers of hubris in the Greek tragedies, our self-involvement brings us only peril in the end. Jeffers would have us be what we are: nerves in the body of the universe, a lightning rod for feeling and experience, and still a tiny part of the whole, in context, not separate. From that frame we can see what is truly important.

*

Civilisation and its ephemera would come to Jeffers' place in his time. As his reputation waned, and the Carmel area became more popular, he was forced over and over to carve away pieces of his land. What remains is just the small lot where Tor House sits, thankfully preserved from a developer who wanted to level it. If you go there now you will see the mansions set right at the property line around Jeffers' walls, the headland built upon in all directions. The transient edifices aching to fall into the sea.

He wrote on it when it first began to happen:

> This beautiful place defaced with a crop of suburban
>   houses –
> How beautiful when we first beheld it,
> Unbroken field of poppy and lupine walled with clean
>   cliffs...

I can feel his pain, anger, disgust. His very home, the place that gave him his deepest understanding of the world, is being *defaced*. There was a time when I longed for the money to buy all this land, sweep it clean of these insubstantial structures.

But Tor House, in contrast with them, has a new meaning. In the long view, these homes rise and fall around it like a wave, or fruiting fungus, soon to disintegrate. The house will remain, a steady point in this landscape, an outcrop of stone.

*

Stand from your place by the window, cross the parlour. Bow your head under the low lintel, enter the next room. Comforting, warm and enclosing, the same dark wood panelling, close ceiling. A large window faces the west, the cobalt ocean. The sun slanting in to rest on the floor.

The guest bed occupies most of the space. Stand at its foot. The brass rail, the bone coverlet. Hear the quiet. Feel him here. He wrote of this room too, that he set aside this bed to die in. It was here he died in January of 1962, having never abandoned his place. An uncommon snow fell on Carmel that day.

Step back, leave that room. Go out through the cottage, into the garden again. Know that he is here, along with Una, their ashes resting beside the wall. In every way, their physical presence is impressed on the place. Hear the waves thunder, feel the buffeting breeze.

Cross the garden to the base of Hawk Tower. How it looms above you, drops its shadow over the garden.

Pull back the heavy door on its wrought hinges. Step into the small cool room, be surrounded by the stone. Here is where they moved his desk, and his chair. It waits for you. Sit down in the heavy seat, feel its smoothed arms circle around you, the space that was meant to hold his frame, all those long hours composing, more than forty years. The broad plane of the desk is before you, darkened with spots of ink. Touch the grain of the wood, feel where he put his hand, where he lay his paper, where he inscribed his words.

Step out of that stone room, climb the steps that wind around the tower's sides, among the branches of the silver-trunk cypress. Come at last to the parapet, the stones beneath you solid and real. Feel his ghost here, deep in the granite. Stand and look out to the vast mirror of the Pacific. If you look down to the shore, you may see me hunched among the striated stones, reading a small book or watching the waves roll in from the west.

Tor House

Robinson Jeffers

If you should look for this place after a handful of lifetimes:
Perhaps of my planted forest a few
May stand yet, dark-leaved Australians or the coast cypress,
  haggard
With storm-drift; but fire and the axe are devils.
Look for foundations of sea-worn granite, my fingers had the art
To make stone love stone, you will find some remnant.
But if you should look in your idleness after ten thousand years:
It is the granite knoll on the granite
And lava tongue in the midst of the bay, by the mouth of
  the Carmel
River-valley, these four will remain
In the change of names. You will know it by the wild sea-fragrance
  of wind
Though the ocean may have climbed or retired a little;
You will know it by the valley inland that our sun and our moon
  were born from
Before the poles changed; and Orion in December
Evenings was strung in the throat of the valley like a
  lamp-lighted bridge.
Come in the morning you will see white gulls
Weaving a dance over blue water, the wane of the moon

Their dance-companion, a ghost walking

By daylight, but wider and whiter than any bird in the world.

My ghost you needn't look for; it is probably

Here, but a dark one, deep in the granite, not dancing on wind

With the mad wings and the day moon.

Notes

1. Jeffers, Robinson, from the Forward, *The Selected Poetry of Robinson Jeffers* (Stanford, California: Stanford University Press, 2001), p.713–718.
2. 'Apology for Bad Dreams', ibid., p.141–144.
3. 'Tor House', ibid., p.181.
4. 'Return', ibid., p.499.
5. 'Apology for Bad Dreams', ibid., p.141–144.
6. 'Tor House', ibid., p.181.
7. 'Poetry, Gongorism, and a Thousand Years', ibid., p.723–728.
8. 'To the Rock That Will Be the Cornerstone of the House', ibid., p.21.
9. 'To the House', ibid., p.18.
10. from the Introduction, *Roan Stallion, Tamar and Other Poems*, ibid., p.710–712.
11. from the Forward, ibid., p.713–718.
12. from the Introduction, *Roan Stallion, Tamar and Other Poems*, ibid., p.710–712.
13. from the Preface, *Roan Stallion, Tamar and Other Poems*, ibid., p.710–712.
14. 'Apology for Bad Dreams', ibid., p.141–144.
15. Ibid.
16. Ibid.
17. Ibid.
18. from 'At The Birth of an Age (a vision of the self-hanged God)', ibid., p.506–507.
19. from the Preface, *Roan Stallion, Tamar and Other Poems*, ibid., p.710–712.
20. 'Meditation on Saviors', ibid., p.172–177.
21. Ibid.
22. from the Forward, ibid., p.713–718.
23. 'Carmel Point', ibid., p.676.

Uncivilised Poetics – Audio Texts

[opposite, and previous] KATIE EBERLE *Limantour II.*
Photograph of Limantour Beach, Point Reyes, California.

Rearmament

Robinson Jeffers

These grand and fatal movements toward death: the grandeur of the mass
Makes pity a fool, the tearing pity
For the atoms of the mass, the persons, the victims, makes it seem monstrous
To admire the tragic beauty they build.
It is beautiful as a river flowing or a slowly gathering
Glacier on a high mountain rock-face,
Bound to plow down a forest, or as frost in November,
The gold and flaming death-dance for leaves,
Or a girl in the night of her spent maidenhood, bleeding and kissing.
I would burn my right hand in a slow fire
To change the future ... I should do foolishly. The beauty of modern
Man is not in the persons but in the
Disastrous rhythm, the heavy and mobile masses, the dance of the
Dream-led masses down the dark mountain.

Roads

George Mackay Brown

(read by Mairi Campbell)

The road to the burn
Is pails, gossip, grey linen.

The road to the shore
Is salt and tar.

We call the track to the peats
The kestrel road.

The road to the kirk
Is a road of silences.

Ploughmen's feet
Have beaten a road to the lamp and barrel.

And the road from the shop
Is loaves, sugar, paraffin, newspapers, gossip.

Tinkers and shepherds
Have the whole round hill for a road.

Durham Beatitude

William Martin

Easington Colliery disaster remembered at
the Durham Miners Gala July 1980

1.

Gorse blazing on clifftop
I saw three ships
Thorns and May blossom
Explosion at pit

I saw three ships
Through the gorse sail in
They came to Death's harvest
They came to pulley-wheels

Saul's Dead March
Common grave and grief
Beatitude their banner
Weeping and drum beat

2.

Candles flicker
in eviction tents

A gentleness flowered
In each drum silence
A Kingdom confronted
Each green thorn

Peppered candymen
Slip on greasy stairs

The Devil's in coal
His horn is a pick

They that mourn
Came here in July
Field blessed with banners
Thronged comforting hush

Hepburn is broken
As old bonds tighten

3.

Quoits ring
Despite gibbet shadow

What Kingdom
Without common feasting?

When they were seated
Silk banners on fellside

Friends after nettle-broth
Turned slogans into bread

By the poor for the poor
They taught themselves

4.

Street children cry Cockerooso
Generations hop across

Spuggie-chorus crack
Cathedral-choir sing anthem

"Our feet shall stand
In thy gates O Jersusalem"

Larks rise with brass
Big Meeting last one for Eden

5.

Pulley-wheel eyes
Haul Ships

White elder sing
Psalms rust to berry

Who sows in tears
Reaps in joy

Clifftop ritual
Picnic-Haggadah

Crushed-Magdalene oil
Gorse-golden vessels

Here and here
Is Jerusalem

Three ships beach
On Shingle spoil

If

Najat Abdul Samad

(transl. Ghada Alatrash)

Wouldn't it have been better if I had emerged as a wild plant in this soil instead of belonging to a family, or if I had been a bundle that was accidentally dropped from above by a passing stork onto a peaceful land that did not have someone I worry about in all four of its directions.

I don't care about being pro or anti. All I want is for my only brother to find food. He is seven years old and is as thin as a shadow, and has not been able to go to school for a day. My fourteen year old sister is also about to collapse from lack of food. And we, the older daughters, have been displaced, each with her husband in a different country. My mother told me that one kilo of rice where they live in al-Ghouta sells for 5,000 Syrian pounds, and that for months they have been under siege, entrapped without electricity, water, work or money. If only I could bring them to me. If only I could send them bread and sugar.

10th March 2014

لو

نجاة عبد الصمد

أما كان خيراً لو أنني انبثقتُ من هذه الأرض نبتةً بريةً لا تنتمي إلى عائلة، أو لو أنّني سقطتُ سهواً من صُرّةٍ كانت بين قدمي طائرٍ عابر، فوقعتُ على أرضٍ مسالمة، ليس لي في جهاتها الأربع مَن أذوب قلَقاً عليه.

لك أنا ما دخلني لا بالموالاة ولا بالمعارضة. ما بدي غير إنو أخي الوحيد يلاقي أكل. عمرو سبع سنين وضعيف مثل الخيال، وبعدو ما قدر يداوم ولا يوم بالمدرسة، واختي ١٤ سنة بتتوقع من طولها لأنه ما في أكل. ونحنا البنات الكبار نازحين كل وحدة هي وجوزها على بلد. إمي قالت لي كيلو الرز عندن بالغوطة بـ ٥,٠٠٠ ليرة ومن شهور محاصرين لا كهربا ولا ميّ ولا طلعة ولا فوته ولا شغل ولا مصاري... لو بقدر جيبن لعندي، لو بقدر ابعثلن خبز وسكر.

١٠ اذار ٢٠١٤

The First Blast to Awaken Women Degenerate

Rachel McCrum

I am assured that God has revealed to some in this our age, that it is more than a monster in nature that a woman shall reign and have empire above man.

And therefore, I say, that of necessity it is that this monstiferous empire of women (which amongst all enormities that this day do abound upon the face of the whole earth, is most detestable and damnable) be openly revealed and plainly declared to the world, to the end that some may repent and be saved.

– *The First Blast of the Trumpet Against the Monstruous Regiment of Women*, John Knox, 1558

The trumpet sounds.
All the monkeys are grooming themselves
    bald
in the zoos

Women slither out from gutters and
    under streetlamps
down from bedsits, and from behind
    garden fences

Foil sail unfolding irresistible as empty
    crisp packets
from pub table women
Women who sink a bottle of red and rage
with wine lips women

Fury unleashed women
in stamping, stomping, sweating
hordes of women

ranks amassing women.

Give me
gorilla women
and bear women
penguin women
and wolf hound women
blue whale women
and badger women
yeti, yak
and bison women

Give me
caribou women
and bone women
bite back
beefy
women

not quite bird women
not least the sparrow
crow
or wren
women
but
flamingo women
peacock women
eagle women
and pelican women

Give me unnatural women
deranged women
moving
drumming
howling women

Give me mobs of women
chow down on misery women
seismic cunt women

bloody pushy women
like a 2 am army's march
through the veins women

Give me ruling women
and yelling women

Give me unsilent unwatchful women
Give me monstrous women
on the pavements of

Cologne women
London women
Tahir Square women
Belfast women
Stockholm women
Cape Town women

Before the second trumpet sounds.
Before the monkeys can groom themselves
        bare and repent
Before the streets can fall dark and silent
        and damned
Please
Give me my monstrous regiment
of women.

Where this poem came from…

The coverage of the 2016 New Year attacks against women in Cologne and Stockholm; further reading about other incidents of mass sexual violence against women, for example, Tahir Square in 2013; the 'corrective rapes' of lesbians, particularly in South Africa; that this is not a phenomenon that happens only outside the UK and Northern Ireland (Dapper Laughs exists, for example); reading *Women Who Run With The Wolves* by Clarissa Pinkola Estes and exploring feminine archetypes around the world; my own feelings – a muscular woman who often feels more akin to a bear than a bird, regardless of what a lot of poetry tells me; the need to free my own voice, to yell and howl and scream against an upbringing that tells me this is uncouth, ugly, excessive; learning about Inuit throat singing, that it is traditionally a female practice, a game, and delighting in how 'unfeminine' and 'ugly' it sounds, and the power that comes from that; my own absolute terror of groups of men, particularly in the streets, of mob think and the violence, the mindlessness, the egging-on that can come from that; my own physical helplessness against those situations, however much I like to think of myself as strong; my need to scream, stomp and rage against that, and my desire to see women able to scream, stomp and rage along with me.

With thanks to Jonathan Lamy, whose vocal support, trust and love enabled this piece to be written.

— RM

Leaving St Kilda

Robin Robertson

Clouds stream over the edge of Mullach Mòr, pouring
into the valley as we sail against the sun from Village Bay,
rounding the Point, and the Point of the Water,
north under Oiseval and the Hill of the Wind, and round
past the Skerry of the Cormorants, the Cleft
of the Sea-Shepherd, and out around the Yellow Headland
to The Hoof, and the Cleft of the Hoof, to The Gap
where the fulmars nest in their sorrel and chickweed;
and on to Stac a'Langa, the Long Stack
also called the Stack of the Guillemot, and Sgeir Dhomnuill,
place of shags, who are drying their wings like a line
of blackened tree-stumps, to Mina Stac and Bradastac
under the deep gaze of Conachair the Roarer
and Mullach Mòr the Great Summit,
and the White Summit and the Bare Summit beyond;
from there to the Cleft of the Leap, of the Ruinous Fall,
and round the promontory, and its tunnels and arches
to Geo nan Plaidean, the Cleft of the Blankets,
and Geo nan Ròn, the Cleft of the Seals, to rest
by Hardship Cave and the deep doorways in the cliffs
of wide Glen Bay; the air still, the Atlantic flat as steel.
Southwards lies Gleann Mòr, the Great Glen, which holds
the Brae of Weepings, the House of the Trinity

and The Amazon's House, The Well of Many Virtues,
and also, it's said, above The Milking Stone, among
the shielings, a place they call The Plain of Spells.
Here also, the home of the great skua,
the bonxie, the harasser: pirate, fish-stealer,
brown buzzard of the sea who kills for the sake of it.
And on past the Cleft of the Lame and the Beach of the Cairn
of the Green Sword and the Chasm of the Steep Skerry
to the crest of The Cambir, and round its ridge to Soay.

Three great sea-stacks guard the gateway to the Isle of Sheep:
the first, Soay Stac, the second, Stac Dona – also called
The Stack of Doom – where nothing lives. The third – kingdom
of the fulmar, and tester of men who would climb
her sheer sides – the Pointed Stack, Stac Biorach.
Out on the ocean, they ride the curve of the wave; but here
in the air above their nests, in their thousands, they are ash
blown round a bonfire, until you see them closer, heeling
and banking. The grey keel
and slant of them: shearing,
planing the rock, as if their endless
turning of it might shape the stone –
as the sea has fashioned the overhangs
and arches, pillars, clefts and caves, through
centuries of close attention, of making its presence known.
Under the stacks, the shingle beach at Mol Shoay,
filled with puffins, petrels, shearwaters, and on the slopes

up to The Altar, the brown sheep of Soay graze.
Above the cliffs, and round again past the Red Cleft
to the rocks of Creagan, Am Plaistir, the Place of Splashing,
under the grey hill of Cnoc Glas, to the Point of the Strangers,
the Point of the Promontory, Flame Point, and beyond that
the Skerry of the Son of the King of Norway.

Back to Hirta and The Cambir to the Mouth of the Cleft
and The Cauldron Pool and down through the skerries
to the western heights of Mullach Bi – the Pillar Summit –
and Claigeann Mòr, Skull Rock.
Between them, the boulder field of Carn Mòr – sanctuary
of storm petrels, Leach's petrels, Manx shearwaters –
and up on the ridge, the Lover's Stone.
Past The Beak of the Wailer, Cleft of the Grey Cow,
the Landing Place of the Strangers, to An Torc, The Boar,
rising from the sea under Mullach Sgar and Clash na Bearnaich,
and The Notches that sit under Ruaival
the Red Fell, pink with thrift – past the white churning
at the mouth of the kyle, and on through the mists
of kittiwakes to the serrated fastness of Dùn:
The Doorpost, The Fank, the Lobster Precipice, Hamalan
the Anvil Rock, The Pig's Snout,
The Fissures, and The Beak of Dùn.

And then north-east, four miles, to the fortress of Boreray,
rising a thousand feet out of the black-finned sea.

To the northern stack: Stac an Armin, Stack of the Warrior,
highest sea-stack in these islands of Britain, where the last
great auk was killed as a witch
a hundred and seventy years ago. On its southern edge,
The Spike, Am Biran, and Broken Point – long loomery
of the guillemot – and across to The Heel,
split vertically in two, and the Cleft of Thunder.
Round, then, the heights of Boreray,
clockwise this time, round
to high Sunadal the swimmy-headed, home of puffins,
and the village of cleits
like turf-roofed chambered cairns
looking down on the Rock of the Little White Headland,
the Bay of a Woman, the Point of the Dale of the Breast,
and round the southern tip of Boreray, Gob Scapanish
– Headland of the Sheaths, Point of the Point of Caves –
and Cormorant Rock and The Cave of Ruin and then
Clagan na Rùsgachan, Skull Rock of the Fleeces,
wreathed in banner-clouds,
the Chasm of the Warrior and the great rift of Clesgor
– to reach, in the west, the Grey Stack, the Hoary Rock,
the gannetry of St Kilda: Stac Lee.
From one side a bishop's piece, from another, a shark;
all sides inches deep with guano you can smell for miles.
A stone hive of gannets, thrumming and ticking
with the machinery of sixty thousand squalling birds.
Off the rock, they open out in perfect cruciform and glide

high over the deep swell to track the shadows
of the mackerel or the herring shoal and then,
from a hundred feet, hundreds of them drop:
folding their wings
to become white javelins –
the dagger bill,
the pointed yellow head,
white body,
white wings tipped black –
they crash
white
into their own white water.

*

All eyes stay fixed
on the great sea-citadel, this
mountain range returning to the waves,
all eyes hold the gaze of the rocks
as the boat turns east – as if
to look away would break the spell –
until a shawl of mist
goes round its shoulders,
the cloud-wreaths
close over it, and it's gone.

At last we turn away, and see them
leading us: bow-riding dolphins,
our grey familiars,
and thirty gannets in a line
drawing straight from Boreray:
a gannet guard
for this far passage,
for the leaving of St Kilda.

Sculpture

Peter Cowdrey

Sculpture was recorded on 11th June 2016, in and around a sculpture by Pierre Vivant near La-Chapelle-en-Valjouffrey in the French Alps. Pierre's piece is made from a massive boulder that had fallen down a nearby mountain onto the valley floor, onto which he painted the French flag, symbol of the local National Park; he then split it into four and jumbled the slices. The main recording was made at midday, when the sound of the Angelus from the village Church resonates through the valley. Shorter recordings of specific sound events made at the site during the afternoon were superimposed on this.

Sound recording at this location is challenging because of the constant roar of three nearby torrents, threatening to engulf all other sounds (the recording site itself was almost obliterated by a weather event last summer). Above the roar can be heard the songs of birds, most prominently blackcaps and chiffchaffs, which are small avian migrants from Africa, and the constant chirping of crickets.

I recorded humans inside the sculpture, a quiet sheltered space with its own acoustic, much used by animals. My sister, Liz Cowdrey, improvised on violin, and she and our friend, Jub, struck stones together, and against the sculpture; stones which had been picked up around the site.

My aim is to explore the lines between human and nature, regular and irregular, local and universal, past and present.

Newsflash

William Letford

Av hud enough
am kickin it in
am packin it up
am maikin a stand
am plantn ma flag
youz kin aw jist go tae fuck

cause thurs too many people
wae too many taunts
who know where thur gon
niver getting wit they want

baws tae bein neck deep
bangin ma heed off a brick waw

Naw

am puntin masel up
it's time tae ascend
it's time tae evolve
am gonnae be immortal
like the stars in the sky
watchin this wee world revolve

inside outside upside doonside backside
frontside
al be the man
an then some mair

when a knoack oan death's door
he's gonnae be feart tae come oot
top eh the food chain?
tell him his fuckin tea's out

Another Great Unconformity
October 2014, NYC

Mark Rylance

A shock the city –
first day after sixteen days
    on the Colorado River
a mile deep in the Grand Canyon
two billion years before today…
Another great geological unconformity.

I stand back while I stand forward.
I eddy while I rush downriver
observing my need to take part,
to be heard, to express my views,
to obtain, to be needed. Why? What need?

I stand also between forward and back,
balancing on a paved walk
that is itself balancing on granite,
deep, dark, quartz-ingrained granite
that is moving between then and now
between form and fluid mineral
and all of us, every cell,
    bound to and born from
this waltzing inner and outer core
of molten compressed star dust.

I stand and collapse the high skyscrapers.
I haystack, boil and whale-rock them down
into the avenues and side streets.
The dam is dismantled and I let my
    imagination empty out
fifty thousand cubic feet per second, more,
roars down the avenues
and swells into the numbered brutal grid.
Debris begins to slide in from the
    cross-streets
and the yellow taxis float and tumble
over narrow gaps in the huge piles
on rapid waves of my imagination.
Long rolling tongues swell uptown
    of these rapids,
and downtown flipped taxis, cars and buses
form submerged or visible, jagged obstacles.
Times Square is a maelstrom
and all the traffic heads one way,
downtown to the ocean.

I see the city collapse completely
and the sea rise and flush it all out,
concrete foundations, steel ambition,
    glassy vanity,
brownstone, penthouse, office floor,
all reduced to a layer of sediment…
No, only a slightly different shade

in a much larger layer of sediment,
a matter of subtle geological pigmentation
in the deposition of half a million years
    of dried beach,
a few inches in a five hundred foot thick
    blanket of sandstone
rolled across the older Mannahatta granite
and industrial Hudson river basin.
All our towering need buried most likely
forever
unless revealed in time to come
by some river canyon, earthquake or shifting
    tectonic plate.
To what? To whom? What for? Why?

My beloved has her hand on my
    naked shoulder,
'You're all right. It's all right,'
    she whispers in the darkness
as my eyes open momentarily
    amidst the engulfing waves
of Sockdolager, Granite, Crystal,
    the dreaded Lava Falls,
rapids, like our present age,
    where each night in sleep
Psyche rows me again
    down Pan's grand canyon.

I stand also now awake
beneath forward and back,
inside my balancing ear,
within the universal darkness.
I see the burning city lights
    obscure the stars –
my travelling companions
    down the Colorado –
Cygnus, the Milky Way, Orion,
    distant Andromeda,
all extinguished above the manmade canyons
and up-lit cliffs of Times Square.
But I know their infinite space is there,
I know they are there always,
older than our earth our sun
but of the same nature, the same dust,
the identical insignificance,
the humble matter
that pools in the hotel bath
when I wash my clothes;
that fills the tiny wrinkled tributaries
and life-line canyons of my sunburnt hand
holding down this page,
while I scratch about and scribble
in another great unconformity.

Baby Scorpion

Francesca Beard

The man put a log on the fire to keep his sweetheart warm.
Out of the bark crawled a baby scorpion.
Long as her little toe, shiny like her hair,
It ran faster than fire, along the burning wood.

'It's a black snowflake,' she said,
And felt pity for its strange symmetry.
It was a knight in black armour on his tiny black charger,
Galloping through a forest of red thorn.
It would not step out onto the bridge of kindling,
Nor would it tuck in the curved lance of its spine.
It would not be saved.

She thought of their bed with its soft dark corners.
She thought of all the insects in the garden.
When it grows up, it will not be small, she thought.
When it grows up, it will be an ugly, dangerous thing.
'Find it and kill it. Make sure it's dead,' she said to her love.
He had green eyes and white teeth.

He found it and killed it.
'Look – it's dead now.'
She went to look at a smudge on the stone.

Out of the stain rose a ghost,
Shaped like a scorpion, but ill-defined.

The girl was afraid. She said –
'I am young and beautiful among my own kind.
I will not harm you unless frightened.
If there is no alternative I will kill myself.
I do not want death forced upon me.
I will come to meet it in all my wildness.'
Then she closed her eyes as if to disappear.
The ghost scorpion was kind.
It killed them quickly.
Left alone, the fire consumed itself and died.

New Mexico Desert Dawn

Bernie Krause

Text for audio piece:

27th April 1992, dawn chorus. Recorded in the panhandle of New Mexico at the foot of the Animus Mountains, Gray Ranch, a 500,000 acre ranch, once owned by The Nature Conservancy, probably the most tranquil recording site I've visited in North America. Geographically, it makes up the meeting place of the Sonoran and Chihuahuan deserts. In over two weeks, we heard only one distant single-engine private aircraft and one automobile. Other than that, just bird and other wildlife unimpeded even by the signatures of domestic animals and humans. Due to good management, this is one of those delicate habitats that has begun to restore itself from nearly four centuries of overgrazing and resource plunder at all levels.

MAT OSMOND Stone #1 *Ink and pencil on paper*
One of a sequence of images made in response to Em Strang's mythopoetic narra-
tive, *Stone*, and published this year as a collaborative chapbook (Atlantic Press, 2016).
Proceeds donated to the Scottish charity Trees for Life.

Acknowledgements

Blanco, Alberto, 'Mala Memoria', *Dawn of the Senses: Selected Poems of Alberto Blanco* (San Francisco: City Lights Books, 1995). Reprinted with kind permission of Robert Sharrard at City Lights Books.

Barghouti, Mourid, 'I Have No Problem' and 'Third World', *Midnight & Other Poems* (Todmorden, Lancs: Arc Publications, 2008). With thanks to Tony Ward and staff at Arc for all their help and support, and for kind permission to reprint.

Capildeo, Vahni, 'Slaughterer', *Measures of Expatriation* (Manchester, UK: Carcanet, 2016). 'Slaughterer' is copyrighted and is reprinted by kind permission of Carcanet Press Limited, Manchester, UK.

Carney, Rob, 'Seven Circles in the Book of Sharks' won the 2014 Robinson Jeffers/Tor House Foundation Poetry Prize and appeared in the Tor House Foundation Newsletter (Summer 2014).

Carruth, Jim, excerpt from *Killochries* (Glasgow, Scotland: Freight Books, 2015). With thanks to Adrian Searle for kind permission to reprint. © Jim Carruth.

Cranston, Edwin, transl., *A Waka Anthology – Volume One: The Gem-Glistening Cup* (Stanford, California: Stanford University Press, 1993). 22 lines of ancient Japanese poetry translated by Professor Edwin Cranston, reprinted with kind permission of Stanford University Press.

Goldberg, Kim, 'Spawn' was originally published in *Imagination & Place: Weather* (Lawrence, Kansas: Imagination & Place Press, 2012).

Haines, John, 'The Owl in the Mask of the Dreamer', *The Owl in the Mask of the Dreamer: Collected Poems by John Haines* (Saint Paul, Minnesota: Graywolf Press, 1996). With special thanks to Fred Courtright for his support. Reprinted with the permission of The

Permissions Company, Inc., on behalf of GraywolfPress, graywolfpress.org.

Haines, John, 'The Tree that Became a House', *News from the Glacier: Selected Poems 1960–1980* (Middletown, Connecticut: Wesleyan University Press, 1982). With thanks to Suzanna Tamminen for kind permission to reprint.

Hass, Robert, 'The Problem of Describing Trees', *Time And Materials: Poems 1997–2005* (New York: ECCO/Harper Collins, 2007). Copyright © 2007 Robert Hass. Reprinted with kind permission of HarperCollins Publishers.

Howe, Marie, 'Annunciation', *The Kingdom of Ordinary Time* (New York: W. W. Norton, 2008). Reprinted with kind permission of W. W. Norton.

Jeffers, Robinson, 'The Beauty of Things', *The Wild God of the World* (Stanford, California: Stanford University Press, 2003). With thanks to Lindsay Jeffers at Jeffers Literary Properties for kind permission to reprint.

Jeffers, Robinson, 'Tor House', *The Selected Poetry of Robinson Jeffers* (Stanford, California: Stanford University Press, 2001). Reprinted by kind permission of Lindsay Jeffers at Jeffers Literary Properties.

Lotfi Gill, Marjorie, 'On Seeing Iran in the News' first appeared in *Acumen 84*, January 2016.

McCaslin, Susan, 'Dank Tureen (a dream about global warming)', *The Disarmed Heart,* (Toronto: St. Thomas Poetry Series, 2014). Reprinted with kind permission of the author.

Martin, William, 'Abuba Bide', *Lammas Alanna* (Newcastle upon Tyne: Bloodaxe Books, 1999). Reprinted with kind permission of Bloodaxe Books.

Must, Emma, 'Notes on the Use of the Austrian Scythe',

CD Acknowledgements

Notes on the Use of the Austrian Scythe (Matlock, UK: Templar Poetry, 2015). With special thanks to Alex McMillen for kindly granting permission to reprint.

Ní Ghríofa, Doireann, 'Chronosequence' first appeared online at *New Dublin Press* 2016, http://bit.do/chronosequence.

Owen, Catherine, 'Litany', *The Wrecks of Eden,* (Toronto: Wolsak and Wynn, 2001). Reprinted with kind permission of the author.

Richardson, Susan, 'Afterworld' was commissioned by World Animal Day 2015 and has been published both on their website and in Issue 3 of *Zoomorphic*.

Ruzesky, Jay, 'The Details – An Interview with Jan Zwicky' was first published in *The Malahat Review* – Green Imagination Issue (#165 Winter 2008).

St. Germain, Sheryl, 'Midnight Oil', *Navigating Disaster.* Copyright 2012 by Sheryl St. Germain. Reprinted with kind permission of Dr Jack Bedell at Louisiana Literature.

Stafford, William, 'A Ritual to Read to Each Other', *Ask Me: 100 Essential Poems* (Saint Paul, Minnesota: Graywolf Press, 2014). Copyright © 1960, 2014 by William Stafford and the Estate of William Stafford. Reprinted with the permission of The Permissions Company, Inc. on behalf of Graywolf Press, Minneapolis, Minnesota, graywolfpress.org

Tranströmer, Tomas, 'A Winter Night', translated by Robert Bly, *The Half-Finished Heaven: The Best Poems of Tomas Tranströmer* (Saint Paul, Minnesota: Graywolf Press, 2001). Copyright 2001 by Tomas Tranströmer. Translation copyright 2001 by Robert Bly. Reprinted with the permission of The Permissions Company, Inc. on behalf of GraywolfPress, graywolfpress.org.

Brown, George Mackay, 'Roads', *The Collected Poems of George Mackay Brown*, eds. Archie Bevan and Brian Murray (London: John Murray, 2005). With thanks to Jenny Brown at Jenny Brown Associates for kind permission to reprint.

Jeffers, Robinson, 'Rearmament', *The Selected Poems of Robinson Jeffers*, ed. Tim Hunt (Stanford, California: Stanford University Press, 2001). With thanks to Lindsay Jeffers at Jeffers Literary Properties for kind permission to reprint.

Krause, Bernie, 'New Mexico Desert Dawn', © 2016 Wild Sanctuary, All Rights Reserved.

Letford, William, 'Newsflash', *Bevel* (Manchester, UK: Carcanet, 2012). 'Newsflash' is copyrighted and is reprinted by kind permission of Carcanet Press Limited, Manchester, UK.

Martin, William, 'Durham Beatitudes', *Cracknrigg* (Durham, UK: Taxvs, 1983). The collection is available as a PDF download at http://bit.do/williammartinpoet

McCrum, Rachel, 'The First Blast to Awaken Women Degenerate', online recording with throat singing support from Quebecois poet Jonathan Lamy: http://bit.do/RMcCrumFirst-Blast

Robertson, Robin, 'Leaving St Kilda', *Sailing the Forest* (London: Picador, 2014). A recording of Robin Robertson reading the poem is included in *Hirta Songs*, his collaboration with Alasdair Roberts. Corrina Hewat plays the harp accompaniment on the audio recording of the poem.

Samad, Najat Abdul, 'If', (translated by Ghada Alatrash), is available online at PBS NewsHour: http://bit.do/NajatAbdulSamadIf. With special thanks to Corinne Segal (Multimedia Editor for PBS NewsHour Weekend) for putting us in touch with Najat and Ghada.

Mountaineers

Ghada Alatrash is a doctoral student at the Werklund School of Education at the University of Calgary. She is a Syrian-Canadian author and translator. Her collection of short stories, *Stripped to the Bone: Portraits of Syrian Women*, was released in May 2016. She co-chairs the Syrian Women's Club of Calgary. One of her causes in life is to amplify the voices of the marginalised through her writings, poetry and translation.

Robert Alcock is an ecologist, writer, designer and builder based in northern Spain. His work has appeared in places including *The Lancet, Poetry Ireland Review, The Land, Permaculture* and *Dark Mountain: Issues 3* and *6*, as well as in two self-published books: *The Island that Never Was: an English castaway in Bilbao* and *Abrazo House: learning in nature.* abrazohouse.org.

Mourid Barghouti was born in 1944 in the mountainous village of Deir Ghassanah, west of the River Jordan in Palestine. He has spent many years in exile, publishing his work in Egypt and Lebanon. In 2003, the first English translation of his work, *A Small Sun*, was published by The Poetry Trust. His most recent collection in English is *Midnight and Other Poems*, translated by his wife, Radwa Ashour (Arc Publications, 2008).

Francesca Beard is a London-based, Malaysian-born spoken word artist who makes interactive and transformational work for live audiences. She has toured her multi-media one-woman shows all over the UK and represents contemporary British culture around the world with the British Council. She's been writer-in-residence at Hampton Court Palace, The Tower of London, The National History Museum, Metropolitan Police and BBC White City. She is currently developing 'Storyverse', a storytelling platform for live and online audiences with B3 Media, and 'A Lie', a new solo show about reality, supported by Arts Council England. Francescabeard.com

Alberto Blanco is one of Mexico's foremost modern poets. He has published some 30 books of poetry, as well as many translations, art essays and childrens' books. Also an artist and musician, he has been the recipient of numerous awards and grants.

Kit Boyd lives and works in London and shows at galleries across the UK. Before becoming a full-time artist, he worked for many years for the Campaign to Protect Rural England and then the Council for the Protection of Rural Wales. He maintains strong links with Mid Wales where he gained his degree in Visual Art and has recently lived. His work follows in the British romantic tradition and is inspired by neo-romantic artists of the 1940s and Samuel Palmer.

Jessie Brennan is a London-based British artist whose practice explores the representation of places through drawing and dialogue, with the people who occupy them.

[opposite] CAROLINE DEAR Trolltinn? *Birch bark and roots*
After a few days on the international artist residency in Kjerringøy, North Norway, I realised that I couldn't ignore the mountains. Trolltinn in particular with its distinctive outline had a very strong presence. What is this presence of a mountain? What is a mountain? In response I made a large wearable 'hat' of local birch bark bound with birch roots in the shape of this mountain, wearing it as part of the opening celebrations and finally placing it on a rock beside the sea and opposite Trolltinn itself.
[photo: Cecilia Jonsson]

She graduated from the Royal College of Art and has exhibited nationally and internationally, including: RESIDENT, City Gallery & Museum, Peterborough; Progress, The Foundling Museum, London; and Coup de Ville, WARP, Belgium. Her project at The Green Backyard is hosted by Metal and supported by Arts Council England, Peterborough Presents, Seedbed Trust, and The Bartlett, UCL. jessiebrennan.co.uk

George Mackay Brown was born in Stromness, Orkney, on 17 October 1921, and died in Stromness on 13 April 1996. He wrote regularly for the local newspaper – articles and essays – and produced several short story volumes, novels, and the poems for which he's best known. He found his inspiration in the eternal cycle of life, and the 'ceremonies of fishing and agriculture' on Orkney.

Jake Campbell has two pamphlets of poetry: *The Coast Will Wait Behind You* (Art Editions North, 2015) and *Definitions of Distance* (Red Squirrel Press, 2012). He is undertaking a PhD in Creative Writing at Newcastle University and divides his time between Tyneside and Chester. jakecampbell1988.blogspot.co.uk

Mairi Campbell is a violist and singer-songwriter. She's a pioneering figure in Scottish music, exploring the interfaces between traditional and indigenous with her voice, songs and viola. Her recent collaboration with Dave Gray has produced the songs and soundtrack to her unique one-woman theatre show, *Mairi Campbell:Pulse*. Mairi was named Instrumentalist of the Year 2016 in the Scots Trad Music Awards. She has previously won Scots Singer of The Year and Tutor of The Year.

Nancy Campbell is a writer and book artist whose work responds to cultural and climate change in polar and marine environments. Nancy's publications include *How To Say 'I Love You' In Greenlandic: An Arctic Alphabet* (winner of a Birgit Skiöld Award) and the poetry collection *Disko Bay*, shortlisted for the Forward Prize for Best First Collection 2016. She is currently touring *The Polar Tombola*, a live literature project documenting the relationship between endangered languages and landscapes. nancycampbell.co.uk

Vahni Capildeo is a British Trinidadian writer who has published five books and two pamphlets, most recently *Measures of Expatriation* (Carcanet, 2016), which was shortlisted for the T. S. Eliot Prize and Forward Best Collection Prize, *Simple Complex Shapes* (Shearsman, 2015), and *Utter* (Peepal Tree, 2013). She is currently travelling and writing non-fiction and poetry on place and the boundaries between the human and the natural, thanks to the Harper-Wood Studentship (St. John's College, Cambridge).

Rob Carney is originally from Washington state in the northwest corner of the USA. He is the author of four books of poems, most recently *88 Maps* (Lost Horse Press, 2015). His work has appeared in dozens of journals, as well as *Flash Fiction Forward* (W. W. Norton, 2006). He is a regular contributor to the online journal *Terrain: A Journal of the Built and Natural Environments*, where his poems and features are archived at terrain.org/tag/rob-carney/. He is a Professor of English at Utah Valley University and lives in Salt Lake City.

Jim Carruth is the current Poet Laureate of Glasgow and has produced six well-received chapbook collections since *Bovine Pastoral* in 2004. He has won numerous awards, including the McLellan Prize and the Callum MacDonald Memorial Award. He is the cofounder and current chair of St Mungo's Mirrorball – the Glasgow Poetry network – and artistic adviser at StAnza, Scotland's international poetry festival. His book *Killochries* was shortlisted for the Saltire Scottish Poetry Book of the Year, the Seamus Heaney Centre for Poetry Prize and the Fenton Aldeburgh First Collection Prize. jimcarruth.co.uk

Charlotte Du Cann works for The Dark Mountain Project as art editor, book distributor and event curator. Her latest book, *Nostoi*, is an exploration of radical mythology. She lives alongside an uncivilised garden in coastal Suffolk. charlotteducann.blogspot.com

Cate Chapman works as managing director of the Ecological Land Co-operative, a social enterprise working to create affordable access to land for small-scale ecological farming in England through the creation of low-impact residential smallholdings. She also manages a small copy editing agency, Skylark Editing. Cate currently lives in a small town on the Sussex coast. ecologicalland.coop

Early in her career, **Maude Schuyler Clay** assisted the photographer William Eggleston. The University Press of Mississippi published *Delta Land* in 1999. Her work is in the collections of The Museum of Modern Art; The Museum of Fine Arts, Houston; and The National Museum for Women in the Arts. *Mississippi History* was published by Steidl in 2016; photographs from the book will be exhibited at the Ogden Museum of Southern Art in 2017. She lives in the Mississippi Delta.

Peter Cowdrey is the founder of Planet Birdsong www.planetbirdsong.org, a global charitable initiative which promotes the use of birdsong for education and communication. A composer and pianist, his current projects include a puppet opera based on *Paradise Lost*, an operatic version of *The Portrait of Dorian Gray*; and *Garden Birds*, a series of short pieces built around slowed-down transcriptions of familiar birdsong with his sister, violinist Liz Cowdrey. Peter also leads birdsong and music walking tours in Andalucia.

Caroline Dear studied botany in Dublin before studying architecture. She worked as an architect and landscape architect in Dublin, Holland, Oslo, London and Paris before moving to the Isle of Skye in 1986 to work and develop her artistic practice. She has received several awards, most recently from ATLAS arts towards researching historic plant structures. She has exhibited and been on residencies in many countries, including Wales, as part of the Flora Project by Oriel Davies, Canada and Finland.

Celebrated as 'a wildfire in a world of fluorescent bulbs' and a 'poetic force of nature', New York City native

Audrey Dimola is a poet, performer, curator, connector and lifelong artist. Her most recent collection of poetry and prose is *TRAVERSALS* and you can find her online at audreydimola.com.

Ann Fisher-Wirth's fourth book of poems is *Dream Cabinet* (Wings Press, 2012). Her other books of poems are *Carta Marina*, *Blue Window*, and *Five Terraces*. With Laura-Gray Street she coedited the groundbreaking *Ecopoetry Anthology*, with an introduction by Robert Hass, published by Trinity University Press in 2013. Former President of ASLE, recipient of senior Fulbrights to Switzerland and Sweden, she is a fellow of the Black Earth Institute. She teaches at the University of Mississippi.

Harriet Fraser is a poet whose practice focuses on environment and culture; she is doing an MPhil at Glasgow University's Centre for Environment, Culture & Communication, and works in the collaborative practice 'somewhere-nowhere' with photographer Rob Fraser (somehere-nowhere.com).'The Wasdale Oak' is one of seven trees featuring in 'The Long View'. thelongview.today

Julie Gabrielli practices and teaches sustainable architecture. Her blog, *Thriving on the Threshold*, explores the territory of living between cultural stories of separation from and/or belonging to the natural world. Her writing, drawings and paintings have been published in magazines including *Ecological Home Ideas* and *Urbanite*, and in *Dark Mountain: Issues 6* and *8* and *Dark Matter: Women Witnessing #3*. She counts on her teenage son and her novel-in-progress for frequent lessons in humility. juliegabrielli.com

Kim Goldberg is busily unmaking myths among the mallards and moon jellies of Vancouver Island on Canada's Pacific coast. She is the author of seven books of poetry and nonfiction, including *Undetectable* (a *haibun* memoir of her Hepatitis C journey) and *Red Zone* (poems of homelessness). She believes that healing the private body cannot be cleaved from healing the planetary body. pigsquash.wordpress.com

John Haines' (1924–2011) books include *For the Century's End: Poems 1990–1999* (2001), *At the End of This Summer: Poems 1948–1954* (1997), and *New Poems 1980–88* (1990), which received a Lenore Marshall Poetry Prize. Haines taught at a number of universities in the USA and received many awards for his work, including fellowships from the Guggenheim Foundation.

Robert Hass teaches literature and environmental studies at the University of California at Berkeley. He is the author of *The Apple Trees at Olema: Selected Poems* and *What Light can Do: Selected Essays*. He is co-founder of River of Words, a programme that encourages children to make art and poetry out of their local environments.

Nick Hayes is a writer and illustrator living in East London. He has published two graphic novels with Penguin Random house: *The Rime of the Modern Mariner* and *Woody Guthrie and the Dust Bowl Ballads*. The third book, *Cormorance*, will be out in the autumn. His website is foghornhayes.com

Robinson Jeffers was born in January 1887 in Pittsburgh, Pennsylvania and died in Carmel-by-the-Sea, California in January 1962. 'One of his favourite poetic themes was the intense, rugged beauty of the landscape set in opposition to the degraded and introverted condition of modern man.' poetsorg/poet/robinson-jeffers.

Neale Jones is a novelist, husband, woodsman and farmhand in southern Oregon. He studied writing at San Francisco State University, and wilderness skills in the Cascade Range. He is at work on a novel set in a dystopian California. To hear his voice in music and writing, visit nealejones.blogspot.com.

Lucy Rose Kerr is an artist living and working in Cornwall. She uses a meditative practice to encourage images to emerge and take form. The works' ambiguous, dreamlike qualities leave a sense of the unknown in sculptural and etched lines, as if drawn with light.

lucyrosekerr.com Jim Carter's poem 'Oath' can be found at jimcartersculptor.co.uk/oath.php

Paul Kingsnorth is co-founder of the Dark Mountain Project. His latest novel, *Beast*, is published by Faber and Faber. paulkingsnorth.net

John Kinsella is the author of many books of poetry, fiction and criticism. He is a frequent collaborator with other poets, critics, fictionalists, artists, musicians, labourers, environmentalists, activists and friends. His most recent volumes of poetry are *Drowning in Wheat: Selected Poems 1980–2015* (Picador, 2016) and *Firebreaks* (W.W. Norton, 2016). His investigation of 'place', *Polysituatedness: A Poetics of Displacement*, is due out with Manchester University Press late 2016. He is a Fellow of Churchill College, Cambridge University and Professor of Literature and Sustainability at Curtin University. But most relevantly, he is an anarchist-vegan-pacifist.

David Knowles edits *Earthlines* magazine with his wife Sharon Blackie, from a small cottage in the hills of Donegal. He is studying and living the Donegal dialect of Irish Gaelic with a growing realisation that the ancient languages of the world have much to teach us. His first poetry collection *Meeting the Jet Man* was shortlisted for the 2009 Scottish Arts Council First Book of the Year award, and a poem from it was Highly Commended in the Forward Prize and included in the 2010 Forward Book of Poetry. Earthlinesmagazine.org

Andy Knowlton is a poet and mixed media artist based in Seoul, South Korea. After graduating from University, he wrote a novel and several short stories, but realising it was hard to get published decided to put his poetry in the public for people to read. He put his poems in coffee shops, inside the books at the bookstore, in the pockets of clothes at the clothing store, in the cracks in the wall, and, in the Drunken Poet's Project, in small bottles held by dolls. andyknowlton.com

Bernie Krause is the author of *The Great Animal*

Orchestra. Since 1968 he has recorded and researched wild habitats across the globe. You can find out more about his work at wildsanctuary.com

Jonathan Lamy is a multidisciplinary poet and performer from Montreal. He is also a poetry and performance art critic, currently postdoctoral fellow at Université Laval. He has published two collections of poetry at Éditions du Noroît, as well as many articles about Quebecois and First Nations poetry. His practice as a performer combines participative reading, sound poetry, poetry-action and intervention in public spaces.

William Letford's debut collection *Bevel* was published by Carcanet in 2012. He has taken part in translation projects through Lebanon, Iraq and Palestine, and in 2014 a chapbook of his poetry, *Potom Koža Toho Druhého,* was translated into Slovakian and published by Vertigo. His work has appeared on radio and television and his second full collection *Dirt* was published by Carcanet in 2016.

Rob Lewis is painter/plasterer by trade, who also writes poems, essays and songs. His writings have been published in the *Atlanta Review, California Quarterly, Cascadia Weekly, Dark Mountain, Poetry Motel, The Southern Review, Whatcom Watch* and others.

Marjorie Lotfi Gill is the Poet in Residence at Jupiter Artland and was the Writer in Residence for Spring Fling and the 2015 Wigtown Book Festival. She is also co-founder of The Belonging Project, reflecting on the flight, journey and assimilation of refugees. Marjorie's poems have been widely published in journals and anthologies in the UK and US, including *Acumen, Ambit, Gutter, Magma, Mslexia, The North, The Reader, Rattle* and *The Rialto,* and have been performed on BBC Radio 4.

The main inspiration behind **Jane Lovell's** poetry is Nature and the indomitable power of Nature, her subjects often viewed through a curved lens. Her work has been published in a number of anthologies and journals including *Agenda, Earthlines, Dark Mountain, Poetry Wales,*

Envoi, the North, Zoomorphic and *Mslexia.* She won the Flambard Prize in 2015 and was recently shortlisted for the Basil Bunting Prize and the Wisehouse Poetry Award.

Garry MacKenzie has won a New Writer's Award from the Scottish Book Trust for his poetry, and is also a winner of the Robert McLellan Poetry Prize. He has a PhD in how landscapes and environmental problems are represented in contemporary poetry. His non-fiction book *Scotland: A Literary Guide for Travellers,* is an introduction to the country's literature, landscapes, history and culture, and was published by I. B. Tauris in 2016.

Andrew Maize is an trans-disciplinary artist based in Lunenburg, Nova Scotia on unceded Mi'kmaq territory. He is involved in collaborative projects such as White Rabbit Arts, the Circus of the Normal and the Lunenburg School of the Arts. andrewmaize.ca

William Martin was born in 1925 in the mining community of Silksworth, near Sunderland. In World War Two he served as a radio engineer in the RAF, and was posted to Karachi. During periods of leave he discovered the Jain temples of Mount Abu and his spiritual journey began. Returning to Silksworth and marrying in 1950, he worked as a painter and then poet. Despite increasing ill health, he continued to write and perform until his death in 2010.

Rachel McCrum has worked as a poet, performer and promoter in Edinburgh since 2012. She is Broad of Rally & Broad, winner of the 2012 Callum Mcdonald Award and the inaugural BBC Scotland Poet in Residence in 2015. Her second pamphlet *Do Not Alight Here Again* was published in March 2015 by Stewed Rhubarb Press, and in 2015, she wrote and performed her first solo show at the Edinburgh Fringe. In 2016, she is CoastWord Writer In Residence, exploring ideas of freeing the voice, feminism and performance in Dunbar..

After spending many years working and studying around the world **Margaret Miller** is now residing in her hometown of Vancouver with her wise and ancient aunt. When not chatting with said aunt or riding her bicycle or studying (still) at Vancouver School of Theology and elsewhere, she spends her time wondering and sometimes writing about how everything fits together, how now relates to then, and what is going to happen next. She is thrilled to be counted amongst the Dark Mountaineers.

Robert Montgomery follows a tradition of conceptual art and stands out by bringing a poetic voice to the discourse of text art. Montgomery creates billboard poems, light pieces, fire poems, woodcuts and watercolours. He was the British artist selected for Kochi-Muziris Biennale 2012, the first biennale in India. Montgomery has had solo exhibitions at venues in Europe and in Asia, including major outdoor light installations on the site of the old US Air Force base at Tempelhof. The first monograph of his work was published by Distanz, Berlin in 2015. robertmontgomery.org

Helen Moore is an ecopoet and socially engaged artist based in NE Scotland. Her debut poetry collection, *Hedge Fund, And Other Living Margins* (Shearsman Books, 2012), was described by Alasdair Paterson as being 'in the great tradition of visionary politics in British poetry.' Her second collection, *ECOZOA* (Permanent Publications, 2015), is a response to Thomas Berry's vision of the 'Ecozoic Era'. natures-words.co.uk

Formerly a campaigner on environment and development issues, **Emma Must** is currently completing a PhD in the Seamus Heaney Centre at Queen's University, Belfast. She won the Templar Portfolio Award in 2014, and her debut poetry pamphlet, *Notes on the Use of the Austrian Scythe*, was published by Templar in 2015. In 2016, Emma was named as one of the 'Rising Generation' of poets by *Poetry Ireland Review*.

Originally raised in Cornwall, **Daniel Nakanishi-Chalwin** has lived, worked and studied for well over a decade in the Yamato region of Japan, the ancient heartland of the nation's poetry. His work has appeared in several issues of Dark Mountain, including *Technê*, the first themed Dark Mountain publication.

Katrina Naomi's poetry has appeared in the *Times Literary Supplement*, *The Spectator*, *The Poetry Review* and on Radio 4. Her second collection, *The Way the Crocodile Taught Me*, was recently published by Seren (2016). Previous publications include *Hooligans*, (Rack Press, 2015), *The Girl with the Cactus Handshake* (Templar Poetry, 2009) *Charlotte Brontë's Corset* (Brontë Society, 2010), and *Lunch at the Elephant and Castle* (2008). Katrina lives in Cornwall and tutors for Falmouth University, Arvon and the Poetry School. katrinanaomi.co.uk

Doireann Ní Ghríofa is a bilingual writer working both in Irish and English. She frequently participates in cross-disciplinary collaborations, fusing poetry with film, dance, music and visual art. Awards for her writing include the Michael Hartnett Poetry Prize, the Ireland Chair of Poetry bursary and a Wigtown Award for Gaelic poetry (Scotland). Her third book *Clasp* was shortlisted for the Irish Times Poetry Award 2016. Doireannnighriofa.com

Jeff Ollerton is Professor of Biodiversity at the University of Northampton, teaching and carrying out research and advisory activities related to the ecology, evolution and conservation of life on our planet. He is particularly interested in pollinator diversity and conservation, and plant reproductive biology. Occasionally he is a poet. Jeff maintains a personal blog at: jeffollerton.wordpress.com

Catherine Owen lives in New Westminster by the Fraser river. She is the author of ten collections of poetry and three of prose. Her latest book is *The Day of the Dead*, short stories from Caitlin press. The poem 'Earth Day' is from a manuscript of ecopoems called *Riven*.

Nina Pick is a founding editor of Mount Vision Press and an editor of the *Inverness Almanac*. She is the author of a chapbook, *À Luz*, recently published by Dancing Girl Press. Her writing has appeared in *Bombay Gin*, *Tule Review*, *Arion*, *Stone Canoe* and *ISLE*, and in various anthologies, including *Dark Mountain: Issues 4* and *7*. She holds a masters in Comparative Literature from UC Berkeley and a masters in Counselling Psychology from Pacifica Graduate Institute. invernessalmanac.com

In 2007, **Tom Pow** was working on a book that became *In Another World – Among Europe's Dying Villages*. He started to write short poems about nests. It took him a while to recognise the link of abandonment. That work became *Nests*, a multi-media collaboration with printmaker, Hugh Bryden, and craft-artist, Lizzie Farey (Royal Botanic Gardens in Edinburgh). *Nine Nests* is a further development of the imaginative world of the nest. It was commissioned as a collaboration with cellist Alex McQuiston and harpist and singer Wendy Stewart for Dumfries and Galloway Arts Festival and has been performed several times since. Tompow.co.uk

Patrik Qvist is a Swedish artist with a background in architecture and land art. His current work revolves around word/text installations in public spaces using cheap and temporary materials like plastic cups and loading pallets. He is working on a book with essays and photos of the world's oldest trees due in 2017. More of his work can be found here: patrikqvist.com

Susan Richardson is a poet, performer and educator whose third collection of poetry, *skindancing*, was published by Cinnamon Press in 2015. Susan is currently Poet in Residence with both the Marine Conservation Society and, World Animal Day. She is the co-founder and poetry editor of *Zoomorphic*, the online literary journal that publishes writing in celebration and defence of animals. Her fourth collection, themed around endangered marine species, will be published by Cinnamon Press in 2018. www.susanrichardsonwriter.co.uk

Alasdair Roberts is a musician based in Glasgow. He is primarily a songwriter/lyricist, composer/arranger and producer, as well as an interpreter of traditional songs and ballads. Over the past 20 years he has released 14 full-length albums of music, most of them through Drag City Records of Chicago. As well as his work with the poet Robin Robertson on the *Hirta Songs* LP, he has enjoyed collaborations with artists from other disciplines, and is a member of the English/Scottish folk group The Furrow Collective.

Robin Robertson is from the north-east coast of Scotland. He has published five collections of poetry and received a number of accolades, including the Petrarca Preis, the E. M. Forster Award from the American Academy of Arts and Letters, and all three Forward Prizes. He has also translated two plays of Euripides, *Medea* and the *Bacchae*, and, in 2006, published *The Deleted World*, a selection of free English versions of poems by the Nobel laureate Tomas Tranströmer.His selected poems, *Sailing the Forest*, was published in 2014.

Jay Ruzesky is a poet and fiction writer whose most recent book is a work of creative non-fiction called *In Antarctica: An Amundsen Pilgrimage* (Nightwood 2013). He is on the editorial board of *The Malahat Review* where he has edited special issues on environmental writing (The Green Imagination Issue) and on the work of poet P. K. Page. He teaches at Vancouver Island University. wordpress.viu.ca/ruzeskyj/

Mark Rylance trained as an actor at The Royal Academy of Dramatic Art (1978–1980). He was the Artistic Director of Shakespeare's Globe Theatre (1996–2006), and has appeared in many films and stage plays, including *The BFG*, *Bridge of Spies*, *Jerusalem* and *Twelfth Night*. Mark is an ambassador of SURVIVAL, the movement for tribal peoples, and a patron of PEACE DIRECT, working for non-violent resolution of conflict. He has co-written two plays, *I am Shakespeare* and *Nice Fish*. He writes poetry for himself, his friends and family.

Dr. Najat Abdul Samad is a Syrian OB/GYN physician. In addition to her degree in Medicine, she holds a degree in Arabic Literature from the University of Damascus. Her publications include *Lands of Exile* and *Syrian Guernicas*. She has also translated and published a collection of Russian short stories into Arabic. She currently lives in Sweida, Syria.

Born in 1914, **William Stafford** published extensively in his lifetime. Amongst his best-known books are *The Rescued Year* (1966), *Stories That Could Be True: New and Collected Poems* (1977), *Writing the Australian*

Crawl: Views on the Writer's Vocation (1978), and *An Oregon Message* (1987). William Stafford died at his home in Lake Oswego, Oregon, on August 28, 1993.

Sheryl St. Germain's poetry books include *Making Bread at Midnight, How Heavy the Breath of God, The Journals of Scheherazade* and *Let it Be a Dark Roux: New and Selected Poems*. She has written two memoirs – *Swamp Songs: the Making of an Unruly Woman* and *Navigating Disaster: Sixteen Essays of Love and a Poem of Despair*. She co-edited, with Margaret Whitford, *Between Song and Story: Essays for the Twenty-First Century*, and with Sarah Shotland *Words Without Walls: Writers on Violence, Addiction and Incarceration*. She directs the MFA program in Creative Writing at Chatham University. sheryl-stgermain.com

Em Strang is a poet, editor and prison tutor. Her writing preoccupations are with 'nature', spirituality and the relationship between the human and nonhuman. Her illustrated pamphlet, *Stone*, (a collaborative work with artist, Mat Osmond) was published in March 2016 by Atlantic Press with all proceeds going to the Scottish charity, Trees For Life atlanticpressbooks.com. Her first poetry collection, *Bird-Woman*, will be published in autumn 2016 by Shearsman.

Tomas Tranströmer was born in Stockholm in 1931, and died there in 2015. A much-loved Swedish poet and writer, his poetry has been translated into over 30 languages and has been honoured by many awards, including the Neustadt International Prize for Literature. His translator and friend, Robert Bly, described him as having 'a strange genius for the image'. In 2011, he was awarded the Nobel Prize in Literature.

David Troupes has published two collections of poetry with Two Ravens Press, and a selection of new work appeared in Carcanet's *New Poetries VI* (2015). He has recently been awarded a Fellowship with the Jerwood Opera Writing Programme to write and develop *Blue Fire*, a science-fiction opera, in collaboration with composer Joel Rust. He is currently completing a PhD on Ted

Hughes and Christianity at the University of Sheffield. See buttercupfestival.com for more information.

Kate Walters studied Fine Art in London, Brighton and Falmouth. She has exhibited in Jerwood Drawing and in many other national selected exhibitions and has taken part in several residencies, including the Isle of Iona (2015–6), the RCA (National Open Art Resident artist) and in 2017, the Isle of Shetland. Interested in sharing the phenomena which illuminate and inspire her, she's given presentations at many UK and European Universities. As a curator, Kate recently brought together a group of artists working with the feminine paradigm called 'Drawing down the Feminine'. Her work is inspired by many poets, especially Rilke, Raine, Mallarme and the raw physical poems of First Nations peoples katewalters.co.uk

Robert Wrigley recently retired from teaching at the University of Idaho. A new book of poems, *Box*, will be published in the USA by Penguin in April, 2017. He intends to write and fish (with flies, for trout) as relentlessly as possible in the coming years. His current project is a collection of essays about the art of poetry, tentatively entitled *Nemerov's Door*.

Jan Zwicky has published nine collections of poetry, including *Songs for Relinquishing the Earth, Robinson's Crossing* and *Forge*. A new collection, *The Long Walk*, which deals directly with ecological cataclysm, is forthcoming in 2016. Her books of philosophy include *Wisdom & Metaphor* and *Lyric Philosophy*, recently reissued by Brush Education, as well as *Alkibiades' Love*, published by McGill-Queens. Raised on the northwest corner of North America's great central plain, she now lives on a small island off the west coast of Canada.

SUBSCRIBE TO
DARK MOUNTAIN

Since 2009, we have made Dark Mountain a home for the work of writers, thinkers and artists exploring the unknown territory beyond the Pale of an unravelling civilisation. This project has taken many forms, but at its heart are books like this.

Everything we have published has been made possible through the support and generosity of our readers. At first, this was a case of hundreds of you joining in with our crowdfunding campaigns. Now, we're asking for a more ongoing form of support.

Take out a subscription to Dark Mountain and you will get each issue as soon as it comes out, at a lower price than anywhere else. You will also be giving us the security we need to continue producing these books.

To read more about the different levels
of subscription, please visit:

www.dark-mountain.net/subscribe

ECOZOA is Helen Moore's response to the destruction caused by industrial civilisation. Her poetry articulates a new future with a powerful, passionate and visionary voice.

"This is nothing less than a declaration of nature's independence, a manifesto for human engagement that is inclusive, respectful and aware of the impact all of us make in our day-to-day lives on the earth's living body... it is a milestone in the journey of ecopoetics." *John Kinsella, poet, novelist & critic*

Helen asks readers not to use Amazon, but instead to buy a copy direct from her publisher Permanent Publications:

www.green-shopping.co.uk/ ecozoa.html

Print subscribers receive FREE digital & app access to our 89 editions / 24-year magazine archive: www.exacteditions. com/read/permaculture

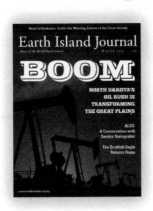

THE LONDON MAGAZINE

Est. 1732

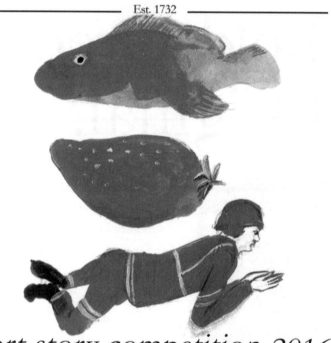

short story competition 2016

opening date: 1st september 2016
closing date: 31st october 2016

www.thelondonmagazine.org

artwork: metamorphose, www.marionkadi.com

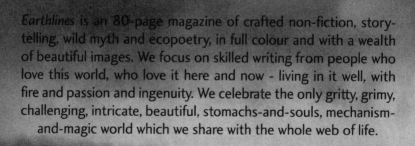

Scottish
Centre
for
Geopoetics

opening a world
expressing the Earth

Stravaig online journal

is available now at **www.geopoetics.org.uk** where you can subscribe to our Newsletter and become a member.

Issues include: Thoreau for today; Coast to Coast: geopoetics in practice; intellectual nomads; geology and geopoetics.

Essays, poems, images, artwork are invited for future issues to nbissell@btinternet.com.

Advance notice: ***Expressing the Earth*: a geopoetics conference** from 22-24 June 2017 in Argyll, Scotland. Call for workshop proposals and more details at www.geopoetics.org.uk.

Geopoetics places the Earth at the centre of experience and expresses it in a wide range of arts and sciences.

Roll of honour

The publication of this book is made possible by the support of subscribers to the Dark Mountain Project. The following subscribers have provided financial support beyond the call of duty. We are very grateful for their belief in our work, and for that of all our subscribers across the world.

Robin Hine

William Johnson

Matthew Osmond

Gregory Webster

Trayton Davis

Paula Boyle

Christopher Hall

Howard Jones

Jennifer Loewen

Gary Krimershmoys

Andrew Junius

Anthony Brown

Peter McDonald

Atlantis Johnson

Matt Leivers

Charles McDougal

Jack Gates Brown

Liz Jensen

Simeon Gallu

Wendy Robertson Fyfe

Nina Ossavy

Jasper M. Mispelters

Ed Luschei

Sara Solnick

Andrew Hurley

Margaret O'Keeffe